A DOG'S EYE VIEW

A CANINE'S THOUGHTS ON HOW TO IMPROVE YOUR WORKING LIFE

BY
BARRY STANNER

A Dog's Eye View: A Canine's Thoughts on How to Improve Your Working Life

Copyright @2018 by Barry Stanner.
All rights reserved under International and Pan-American Copyright Conventions. Published in the United States of America by Parker Productions. No portion of this book may be reproduced, stored in a retrieval system, or transmitted in any form or by any means, electronic, mechanical, photocopying, recording or otherwise, without the written permission of the author. Contact: BarryStanner@gmail.com

ISBN 978-0-578-43140-6 assigned
Non-fiction book: humor in business, A Canine's Thoughts on How to Improve Your Working Life, dogs at work, Vizslas, horse advisor, Paso Finos, Barry Stanner, Pam Stanner, business self-help, improve your working life, canine consultant.

Cover Illustration by Debbie Allen

TABLE OF CONTENTS

PROLOGUE	2
INTRODUCTION	4
THOUGHT ONE: *Relaxez-vous* ~*Stress Reduction*	8
THOUGHT TWO: PPs and PUs: Personal Patterns and Personal Understandings ~*Self-Awareness and Relationships*	22
THOUGHT THREE: Barking Mad ~*Communications*	36
THOUGHT FOUR: 'bout Time for a Treat ~*Expectations*	44
INTERLUDE: Bone Break	56
THOUGHT FIVE: Gotta Scratch That Itch! ~*Ethics*	62
THOUGHT SIX: Hmmm—Who's in Charge? ~*Leadership versus Management*	72
THOUGHT SEVEN: Herd Selection ~*Employment*	88
THOUGHT EIGHT: Get That Bone! ~*Strategy, Tactics, and Implementation*	102
THOUGHT NINE: Please Don't Bite Me! ~*Respect*	112
THOUGHT TEN: My Bones Are Aching for Bones ~*Payment Systems*	120
THOUGHT ELEVEN: Treats, Treats, and Even More Treats ~*Reward Systems*	132
THOUGHT TWELVE: To Sniff, or not to Sniff, That Is the Question ~*Instinct*	138
THOUGHT THIRTEEN: I'm Stuck on You ~*Loyalty*	142
THOUGHT FOURTEEN: My Nose Is Twitching ~*Sensitivity*	146
THOUGHT FIFTEEN: The Last Lick	148
ACKNOWLEDGEMENTS	156
ABOUT THE AUTHOR	164

Contributors Katie, Reign, and Parker

*In memory of Bobby Drinnon, an extraordinary man who
brought guidance, comfort, and hope to countless people.*

*To my wife Pamela, who supported and helped through
all the trials of writing my first book with love and patience.
Pam has been my touchstone throughout the whole process.*

Prologue

Why do you act the way you do? Why do others act the way they do? What do you believe you were put on this earth to do? Do you even ponder what an amazing gift life can be? Do you ever worry about which direction your career is taking? Do you ever wonder if you could have more fun at work? If you aren't having fun at work, why not? What, if anything, can you do to change this situation?

These are just a very few of the many questions that most of us ask ourselves as we journey through our life—at play and at work. Sometimes the answers to the simplest questions can be complex; sometimes the most complex questions yield simple answers. Unfortunately, there are very few simple answers to most *philosophical* questions.

The answer to the ultimate question of "What is the meaning of life, the universe, and everything?" according to a computer built to answer this question in *The Hitchhikers Guide to the Galaxy*, is 42. And who is to say this is not the right answer? Surely the real answer lies within ourselves—if only we will search for it.

This book is a lighthearted series of observations and thoughts that Parker, a Vizsla dog, makes about human behavior when at work. Parker shows that work can be a pleasant place if you will just try to change your approach to the way you think about things, yourself, and others. He offers his solutions by comparing how animals will behave in similar circumstances. Parker provides some insight into how and why we often act the way we do, and what we can all do to improve. He uses animals, with their straightforward approach to life, as examples of how these improvements can be made. Animals have much to teach us humans if only we are prepared to observe, listen, and learn.

Estimates suggest that the average full-time working man or woman spends one-third of his or her life sleeping and one-third working. That leaves just one-third left to us on this planet for free time. If we are to live life to the full and enjoy the all-too-brief period of our current existence, then surely enjoying ourselves at work should be a priority for all of us.

One recent poll showed that in America less than 10 percent of people in full-time employment love their jobs. Parker's objective is to have 80 percent of humans enjoying their jobs—with people impatient to get to work for yet another fun-packed day.

Parker believes we owe it to ourselves and others to constantly learn and improve—and that by so doing this leads the way to a happier life at work and at play.

Introduction

The weather today is chilly—with light snow showers forecast for late morning. There is not a cloud in the sky. The heavens are a shade of wonderful bright blue that can only be seen at daybreak, when the air is clean and fresh. The ground, plants, and bushes are shimmering in the sun, covered from the light frost of last night and shining a hazy gray. This is a beautiful early spring morning in Tennessee—one of those days that makes you glad to be alive.

Our house sits next to the fourth fairway of a golf course. The yard is surrounded by bushes, conifers, and trees that provide privacy when we sit out on our patio to enjoy the sun's warm rays during the summer. In the center of our yard, drifting and weaving down from just below the grass that leads to the fairway, sit two stream beds that flow into a moderately sized pond next to the patio. There is nothing more restful than to hear the soft gurgle of the water rushing past the stones in the streams before splashing delicately into the pond. The water is cold from the harshest winter we have experienced for many years, and our fish are moving as though their fins are still stiff from when the pond was almost frozen over.

I shiver slightly but I have a job to do, so I race to the top of the grassy hill in our backyard. I know that with any luck I can collect some of the wayward balls hit into our yard by the less-skilled golfers. Darn! No success today! I guess the cold weather has kept away the fair-weather players. My niece, Reign, and her beautiful daughter, Katie, join me. We all quickly agree: It's a little too cold to stay out for long. Besides, it's time for breakfast: Our favorite meal of the day! Reign and Katie also know that I was tasked to write this book several years ago by a dear friend of ours. I have procrastinated long enough. This book will be written in his honor—and today is the day to make a start.

With a sigh I turn toward the house and scamper in out of the cold. As I dash past the window I can see the gray hairs on my chin showing sharply in my reflection—and I'm not even 8 years old!

By the way: I'm Parker, a Vizsla dog. Reign and her daughter Katie are both bitches of our proud breed. Just to be clear: I'm talking gender here rather than temperament. For those not familiar with our breed of dog, we are Hungarian pointers. Vizslas are short-haired, regal, loving, and gentle of manner. We have a solid golden-rust coat, and even our noses, eyes, and toes blend in with this color to give us a distinctive, haughty look. We are often called the "Velcro dogs" because we always stick close to our companions. We are energetic, enthusiastic, charismatic, extremely smart, very handsome, brilliant in most things that dogs like to do—and, above all, extremely modest!

Reign, Katie, and I live with two human companions, Pam and Barry. They serve us well, and generally seem to understand what we like to eat, when we want to go out, and when we like to stroll through the well-manicured streets in the gated community where we live.

My full kennel name is Lorac's Parker's Pleasure. My lovely niece Reign is Lorac's Smoky Mountain Reign, and her daughter Katie is Lorac's Chasing Reign-Bows. People often ask me how I came by my name. Believe it or not, my name comes from a famous science fiction series, *The Thunderbirds*, shown on BBC-TV in the 1960s. One of the stars of the show was Parker, the butler and chauffeur to an aristocrat-turned-secret agent named Lady Penelope. Parker was a London cockney who was rescued by Lady Penelope from a background of crime. Like me, Parker was modest, loyal, faithful, dependable, extremely lovable, and, despite his criminal past, very honest. Had I been born a girl you will not be surprised to know I would have been called Lady Penelope!

I am responsible for Pam and Barry—and that is not an easy job. My burden over the years has been to listen to, and witness, all the problems humans face in leading their everyday lives, especially those things associated with work. "Work," it seems, is a place of misery for so many, and a place where some humans are in constant pain or distress.

I really want to help these poor, tortured, and unhappy souls. This is the main reason I committed to writing this book. In my humble opinion, life just doesn't have to be that difficult.

I have collected a series of observations and thoughts, so I can guide at least some humans toward a place of peace and enlightenment. As I write my stories I realize with ever-increasing clarity just how more balanced animals are than our two-legged companions.

It seems to me that mankind has a great deal to learn from us if only they will take time to listen to what we have to teach them. A very wise friend once told me, "Parker, when humans are ready to learn the lesson, the teacher who can teach them will appear in their lives." If this is true, and it might be, perhaps *I am* supposed to write this book after all! So here goes: Advice from me, Parker the dog, on how you can put enjoyment and fun back into your working life. Let's have fun together and go chase that ball!

PARKER

THOUGHT ONE

Relaxez-Vous
~ *Stress Reduction*

My first observation, as a purebred, proud, handsome, self-effacing Vizsla, is that you guys have major problems when it comes to knowing how to relax. You always seem to be in a hurry—even if you are planning on doing nothing! Dogs, on the other hand, understand completely how to relax. We are always searching for comfortable spots to bed down so that we can sleep stress-free while being kissed by the sunshine and cooled by a breeze.

Why do I think you don't know how to relax? Have you ever watched another human getting ready for work? I'm trying to rest after a nice morning walk and you are all scampering about like a puppy looking for a lost tennis ball!!! You run around trying to complete too many tasks in too little time—and then you complain about how stressed you are!

And what about *after* work? I have observed *my* companions arrive home from work and then rush through chores—and that includes taking us outside for a bathroom break before feeding and watering us. Why are they in such a hurry? They also take care of their own daily routines such as cooking, eating, cleaning, and bathing. Then they plop down in a chair to watch television—a mystical box that appears to take away their ability to think and feel. Sometimes I hear them moan and groan about the stresses they had to endure during their day at work. Eventually they fall asleep—just in time to wake up to go to bed.

Sometimes my humans blow through the door like an Arctic wind, complete their chores, and then fly out the door again to play sports or go to a place they call "the gym." This gym must be another place of torture where great pain is meted out by someone called a "personal trainer." My companions, Pam and Barry, attend something called "Yoga." Certain types of Yoga can be another source of pain, but I've been told that it does include nice long rest periods in the midst of all the strange stretching. Pam and Barry's Yoga is Svaroopa, which I hear is very gentle and concentrates on reducing tension within the body. Barry calls it "old person's yogurt," which he finds amusing. Pam never chuckles, though, so I am not sure if this is funny.

If my companions do not go to the gym or attend a class, they often dine at a restaurant—no scraps for me—and gorge themselves on what they refer to as "high-calorie foods." This obviously makes them feel guilty because they immediately start patting their stomachs and making arrangements to go back to the gym.

Barry is classified as an "over-achiever." Partly this stems from the fact that he always wants to do more than he can possibly accomplish, partly because his pride pushes him to do more than someone else, partly because he is a stubborn perfectionist, and partly because he doesn't know any better. He calls it "being competitive," and sometimes this is true. But when he has five jobs on the go at once, or when he "overdoes" it in the garden or on some project and complains he's hurting as a result, he drives poor Pam to distraction.

A classic example of "overdoing things" is when Barry had his hip replaced. The operation went amazingly well. Within a very short time he was almost walking normally and impressing everyone with his speed of recovery. Then he went to physical therapy and the practitioner happened to comment about the problem Barry was having with leg raises. Perhaps he should push a little harder. Red rag to a bull! Soon the leg was repetitively rising to the ceiling despite the intense pain with Barry biting pieces out of the treatment table. Result: a treatment table bearing the scars of war, a pulled muscle, and a three-week setback on the recovery path. Sigh! All we could do was to cuddle up to Pam in sympathy as she muttered something about "men" and "stupidity."

But the real over-achieving mode for most people stems from how they approach work. Many of you set unobtainable goals or objectives that have to be met with a timetable that leaves no time for relaxation or fun. Setting the "bar" high for achievements to be reached is an admirable thing to do. Without some sort of plan and an idea of how to get there objectives will not be met—but trying to do too much too quickly is the equivalent of running into a brick wall at full speed. Having bounced off a few times you might get the message that it hurts. Doing it repeatedly is ill-advised. Albert Einstein is commonly credited with saying that the definition of insanity is "doing the same thing over and over again and expecting different results."

Leaps of faith are usually necessary at some point in all our lives. That leap may mean trusting yourself or others to do something that is outside of your comfort zone. You may decide to change career path, or your company, or even your personal circumstances. Don't ignore your instincts or feelings if your gut is screaming at you for change! Regret at not doing something is one of the worst emotions to have as you journey through life. You can torture yourself in later years with the words, "if only I had … ." I well remember the time that I had the opportunity to pick up a nice juicy bone when no one was looking and … but that's a tale for another time.

Be careful, though, not to make leaps of faith for leaps of faith's sake. You can research and be careful in what you do and still make credible leaps. Foolish leaps into the dark in the hope that something will turn out for the best is just that: foolishness. If your instinct is telling you strongly that you need to take action, it's probably for a reason—and will usually turn out to be the right decision.

Stress can come in many forms, either real or imagined. Take, for example, the ultimate stress maker: visits with friends or family. These should be fun times but often just the thought of making these visits can cause tension. I can feel the concern and dread in my own companions as arrangements are made for such gatherings, especially for "holiday" celebrations. I love seeing other dogs—particularly other Vizslas—so I don't understand why such interactions can cause irritation, anger, envy—and even frustration!

Most of the time we three gorgeous creatures are left at home to rest while our companions leave to "enjoy" themselves. Having anticipated the worst before the visit (and getting stressed out), most of the time my friends return home saying what a wonderful time they had.

I have to admit: Sometimes things don't go well and Pam and Barry return irritable and angry. I've even heard a friend of ours say "the law of averages states that we can expect a pretty horrible time." From what I've read, however, the "law of averages" is not a proper science at all, and certainly not borne out from empirical measurements. For example, most people think that if you flip a coin 100 times, the coin will repeatedly have a "50/50" chance of coming up "heads" or "tails." In fact, studies have shown there is only an 8 percent chance this will happen!

My advice: Don't expect a bad outcome from these events. Approach the events with a positive frame of mind. If all the participants have a negative attitude then it should not be a surprise if a good time is not had by all. On the other hand, if everyone turns up to enjoy themselves, the chances are much greater that the gathering will be a success. I always try to "go with the flow," as they say, and wag my tail at everyone. Trust me: People admire and embrace positive thinking, and most will react in kind. Nearly always my enthusiasm and love for all gets me cuddles, pats, and (when I'm lucky) treats.

Pam's animal therapy and wellness business includes energy work for the animal client. Once an assessment has been completed to identify any issues, Pam sets her intention for the outcome of the treatment. If an animal has an incurable condition it may not always be possible to simply say, "I will cure this poor soul," and she cannot prevent animals from getting old. Pam always asks for help in making the client as comfortable and pain-free as possible so that they can enjoy the best quality of life. Her intention is always for the "highest good of the animal." Unlike humans, animals have no preconceived ideas or resistance to treatment, and most will simply absorb Pam's ministrations as a gift from the unseen. The results are quite remarkable to behold.

If Pam can help animals to have a better, more enjoyable life—and much of her work helps the animal to heal from within itself—then what if humans could set their intention to enjoy their work each day, to be generous to their fellow employees, and to add as much value as they possibly can to the company. I cannot help but wonder if humans' lives would improve exponentially if they went to work each day with such positive intentions.

Barry mentioned today that he went to his favorite coffee bar and the guy working the till was not a happy bunny. The employee's attitude toward Barry conveyed irritation and the employee's responses were short and clipped. Barry made his order simple to avoid irritating this gentleman even more. When Barry reached the end of the bar to pick up his coffee, the girl was bright, cheerful, and asked him how he was doing. When she passed the elixir in a cup to Barry, she asked that he taste the coffee to ensure the order met his expectations. She made Barry feel that he was a respected customer and she wanted him to be satisfied with the product. The bottom line for me was that one employee did little for himself, the company, or the customer, while the other employee achieved a far more satisfactory result in all departments.

I love puppies and have great fun playing with them, but when humans have children I have to confess that planning a schedule can be more problematical. Sometimes the opportunity for the adults to have fun can be greatly reduced when little ones are involved. That said though, there can be no greater joy than seeing puppies (sorry, I mean children) having a wonderful time. When puppies come to see me, I start to get all my toys out for them. My advice here is to try to think ahead a little and have ideas about how the children can play while the adults get together. It may not always work, but most times both adults and children will have a more enjoyable time.

A friend of ours that we see from time to time, and who used to work with Barry, organized amazing events for the children when they visited her house. Without doubt the children always wanted to "go see Aunty Karen." There were no whining kids when the parents set off to visit with this family. On the contrary, it was more a case of "Are we there yet?" What if you could apply these thoughts to work?

In her professional life, Karen often organized events for the employees. Everyone looked forward to attending. People talked to each other and got to understand more about their colleagues and co-workers. I attended a couple of the festivities and loved them because of all the attention I was given. The scraps of food people surreptitiously gave me when they thought Barry wasn't looking helped cement my fondness for the celebrations. I like the word "celebrations" because that was how they were regarded—as celebrations of being together and working for the same company.

The result was a community spirit that helped improve the working environment for all. I don't believe a once-a-year company-sponsored picnic cuts it! Employees feel obliged to attend, and often regard these affairs with suspicion. Most feel they are a waste of money and would rather see the cash in their back pocket. Events to bring people closer together, however, do not need to be expensive, or extensive, to be effective. Regular and relaxed gatherings given for no particular reason yield great results! Most people are more than happy to give up a lunch hour for such events. As Barry used to say, "The way to an employee's heart is through their stomach." It certainly works for me!

Let's talk a little about some of the ways humans seem to try to "relax." I understand why you all want to "do nothing but chill out," but many of you appear to seek places away from your home that cost a lot of money. Is spending a lot of money relaxing?

We dogs understand money to be a unit whose main task originally was to allow exchange of metal and paper for food or some other practical goods. Nowadays most people want to accumulate money so that they can buy things they don't need (but have convinced themselves they absolutely have to own) or go on vacations they cannot really afford. It's true, is it not? We Vizslas are proud of our native intelligence.

When you arrive at your vacation place of substantial expense, you examine your surroundings in a very critical fashion and complain that the hotel room and facilities do not live up to the expectations of the fantastic description you saw on the Internet. For example, the brochure described "an exclusive beach where the soft, white sand caresses your feet as you stroll idly along the shoreline while waves lap gently at your feet." Why would you think that the beach is totally exclusive to only you? Well, the beach is exclusive—to you and 500 other hotel guests! The beach is isolated and the sand *is* soft (I just *love* soft sand on my paws!!!)—and used to be white before the oil slicks arrived. The beach is only 15 yards long and the Internet brochure "forgot" to mention that for 11 months of the year the waves crash in like roller coasters. But what did you expect for 40 percent off?

I've seen humans pursue many activities in order to make themselves feel better. For example, I've seen bits of plastic clipped to your feet! You spend many hours going up a snow-covered hill—and then you go down the hill on your plastic-covered feet! You repeat this process many times while trying not to hit trees, rocks, ice, or another human. You end up sweaty and exhausted. And this is called relaxing!

I know many of you don't like putting the plastic on your feet. Some of you don't even venture out into the snow—but at the end of the day everyone joins up in a lounge with a big fire. There you enjoy something called "après ski." This involves drinking liquids that make you dizzy and you laugh a lot for no reason. Sometimes you fall over and someone has to put you to bed. Then you wake up the next morning moaning and groaning—just like the days when you are getting ready for work—but you say you had a great time the previous night (even though I can tell you don't remember anything!). Most odd!

What's really strange, too, is the amount of stress you undergo when preparing for your vacation. Stress before and stress after! You can understand why we dogs sometimes have difficulty relating to human issues.

I do agree, though, that some of these wild activities do force you to give your brain a rest from thinking about work. How can you consider what your boss is demanding of you at work when you are busy trying to keep from drowning because you have not been swimming since the previous year, or you are trying to avoid a tree that has unreasonably stepped into your path on the ski slope? Perhaps you should actually step up some of these activities *now*—and not just during a vacation?

During my time with Pam and Barry, I have found that many of you spend an unnatural amount of time at work—and then you come home and spend hours talking about your day! I have heard Barry say that he even knows people who dream about work! Pam says some of their friends "live to work rather than work to live," and that if they don't change their approach to life they will die young.

I'm not quite sure what all this means, but I do know that overdoing it at "work" seems to add a lot of tension and stress to your lives. In some cases, stress can even cause you to become sick. Work and stress certainly make you cranky and irritable. What's the point of all that work if you are too tired or too sick to play with me when you come home? I love to play!

I live to play and play to live. I can only play for so long though before I become tired, at which point I just sit or lie down. Consider if you could learn to do this with work. Work until you feel you've had enough, and then go home. I understand that many people have no choice in their working hours, but if you manage people take note of someone who is beginning to tire and let them go home or take a break. Encourage them (and yourself) to take regular breaks, take regular vacations, and take their time.

Yes, I know you will come across people who will try to take advantage. If they do, let them take up employment elsewhere. One way or another you will reach that point with these individuals. Imagine if everyone could enjoy their work with enthusiasm like I do with play— and could find a way to balance their playing with work.

You will hear this from me many times, but I make no apologies for repeating myself. When you enjoy your work, you will work to enjoy yourself. In other words, when work is no longer a tedious task you will find the quality of your work will be higher, your spirit will shine (you will infect others with your happy mood and enthusiasm), and you will be at your maximum efficiency. You will find it easy to get up in the morning—don't tell me you haven't leapt out of bed to go do something you really want to do because you enjoy it—and you will find your sense of self-satisfaction and pride in accomplishment at an all-time high. No time for gossip! No time to complain about your boss, the company, or your work! No thinking about changing your job! (Employers: Please note this is definitely to your advantage!)

Need proof? I believe we all know dog owners who are less than kind to their animals. Watch a dog who has a mean owner next time it is asked to perform a task. The dog will do what it is told to do so that it can avoid punishment, but its tail will be between the legs, the head will likely be down, the movements will be slow, and when the task is completed the dog will either sit or lie down. Now think of a dog who is asked to do something it enjoys. I love going to agility or sheep dog trials. The dogs can hardly control their enthusiasm for what's ahead. When they run their movements are full of energy, their love for what they are doing is plain for all to see, and the look of satisfaction and enjoyment when they have completed their work shines through their eyes.

An inability to relax can make you moody. That is not fun! Much of the time you are pleased to see your pets when you come home from work or from one of your activities. You enter the house smiling, holding your arms open wide and speaking a funny language in a pleasant voice. I've heard you say things such as, "How are our little funny duddy wuddums?" and "Have you been good doggy woggies?"

Sometimes, though, you arrive home mad as a hornet (I, for one, by the way, don't like bees, hornets, or wasps), complaining about something that has happened at work, about some motorist that cut you off in traffic, or some other issue that has upset you. When you want us to come into the house from the yard you speak a lot louder, harder, and deeper. I don't like this. Sometimes Barry will scold Reign,

Katie, or me. Barry will complain, "Will you danged dogs stop jumping all over me? What's wrong with you?"

I like the *pleasant* voice. When Reign or Katie or I hear the nice voice, we jump up and down and wag our tails gleefully—since this seems to meet Pam and Barry's need to be wanted and loved. However, when they use the louder, harder, deeper voices, we tend to tuck our tails between our legs and try to find somewhere to hide. To paraphrase one famous American president who wore a tall hat, "You can please some of the humans some of the time, all of the humans some of the time, but you can never please all of the humans all of the time."

To illustrate how good we dogs are at pleasing humans, a friend of Pam and Barry's often challenges other friends to put their wives and dogs in the trunk of their car for 10 minutes and then see which one greets them enthusiastically when the trunk is reopened.

Barry, who is an American now, but was originally a Brit, retired recently. My understanding is he does not need to go to work anymore. We Vizslas of Hungarian descent, however, do not hold Barry's British heritage against him. As mentioned earlier, we are very well-mannered animals. We are trying, though, to understand more about his ideas on retirement.

At first, I thought this "retirement" would mean more play between us. I was so looking forward to longer walks and more treats! Since Barry gave up work, however, he is busier than ever, filling his day with even more activities and projects than he had when he was employed. He complains he "never has a spare moment"—and this reaffirms my prior statements about humans not knowing how to relax.

Whenever anyone asks Barry how he is getting on, he always replies that he just doesn't understand how he ever managed to fit work into his schedule. The first time he said it we were amused, but this tune soon got very old.

Before retiring Barry was a "Vice President," but which vice he presided over was never clear to any of us. When asked by other dogs what Barry did for a living all day, we simply said, "He doesn't do anything! He's a manager!" Everyone nodded—so I guess we had it right!!!

The Dog's Eye View, or D.E.V. for those of you who love acronyms, is that the Surgeon General really should insist that many letters of employment carry the warning: "Stress of working at this facility can seriously damage your health."

If dogs could talk we would tell humans several things you can do to reduce stress both at work and in your lives in general:

The majority of you are in control of stress. If you truly want to reduce stress you need to change your attitude, approach, or perhaps even your job. Some stress can be necessary and should be viewed as positive since it drives us to achieve results in an acceptable time frame. For some animals, stress can be a life saver, such as when danger threatens and action may be necessary. This kind of short-term stress, though, rarely harms our body. It is the long-term persistent stress that seems to do the damage. If stress begins to affect your health, who you are, or how you react and treat others, then change is essential.

Most animals will not accept stress and will either adapt to the circumstances or make changes. In general, humans have more choices than animals as far as stress is concerned. From the canine pet point of view, we are often at the mercy of how our companions look after us. A dog's love is unconditional. Even when treated inappropriately most dogs will continue to forgive and love their companions. This is true for many animals, although some wild animals may be driven to hide or run away once they understand they will be hurt or killed by humans. Others may become aggressive, often out of fear. We may not always be able to communicate our distress and we may forgive quickly—but there is no acceptable reason for animal cruelty.

If others are applying stress in a way unacceptable to you then you should change your approach or eradicate these folks from your life. If a dog does not like another dog we either fight or simply walk away from each other—once the growling and barking is over. At work you guys sometimes accept that your boss can place as much stress as they like upon you because they are the "boss."

It is possible that your immediate superior is unaware of the unwanted pressure he or she is applying. Try discussing how you feel with your supervisor if you believe you are unable to give of your best because of constant pressure or stress. Try not to be aggressive, however, since this will only make the other person feel defensive. If your manager is not very approachable, or you feel uncomfortable speaking to them directly, consider using other ways to discuss your concerns. Performance reviews, for example, can be an excellent time to have "heart-to-heart" discussions to clear the air. If the supervisor is simply a bully then talk to the bully's superior. Should this not provide a satisfactory result you may have no option but to change your job—if this is a possibility.

Barry often refers to the method he was taught to use to reduce tension when working in the United Kingdom. If something difficult or sensitive needed to be discussed, the meeting would be adjourned to the local pub. The principle was that this was neutral territory, other people were around, and it was far more difficult to become angry, abusive, or aggressive with a pint of beer in your hand. If the discussion was of a personal nature then it was best to consume several pints to ensure the conversation was appropriately lubricated. Sometimes, the next day, neither party could remember exactly what conclusions had been reached the night before, but everyone knew that somehow the subject had been satisfactorily closed. Hmmm—I'm not sure this would work in certain parts of the United States: Not enough pubs!!!

 Why not create a relaxed atmosphere in neutral territory? Barry had a settee and comfortable chairs in his office so that guests, customers, or employees could chat in an informal fashion. Coffee, tea, water, and treats were often on the agenda. Comfort, food, and drink always put people at ease.

I would strongly advise against trying to mimic people who create stress for others or trying to "get your own back" on the stress makers. The worst thing you can do is to lower yourself to someone else's standard. If your own standards or values are higher than those who create unnecessary stress, believe it or not you will add even more stress ¬to your life if you lower yourself to their level. Do not become that which you despise.

When I'm in the car with Barry and some idiot driver cuts him off or performs some dangerous act of driving, he tries to resist the urge to retaliate by saying, "I will not lower my standard of driving to that clown." Occasionally he says this through gritted teeth. That's not to say he will always let the act pass unnoticed—as sometimes he will use his car horn or flash his lights politely to show his disapproval.

Animals never lower their standard of behavior to that of the lowest-performing creature. At one point I have to confess I did consider making cats an exception to the rule of "non-retaliation." I abandoned the idea when I realized that would be an example of me lowering my standards. Besides, cats come armed with sharp, defensive weapons. The thought was very tempting though!

Another suggestion to lower stress is to get a pet. When you get home from work you can put all your frustrations or tensions to one side by loving us—because a pet will love you back. Particularly if you play with us and offer tasty treats. Recent studies have shown that owning, and loving, a dog can prolong the life of a human by up to seven years.

As Cesar Millan, star of the television show, *The Dog Whisperer*, once said, "The dog is a reflection of your energy, of your behavior. You have to ask, 'What am I doing?' That's the right question to ask."

THOUGHT TWO

PPs and PUs: Personal Patterns and Personal Understandings
~ *Self-Awareness and Relationships*

We delectable and cuddly canines always like to start with the basics. Pam and Barry were talking about me writing this book with Denise, a friend who has a wonderful crystal shop in the delightful town of Hawi on the Big Island of Hawaii. Denise suggested Pam and Barry make sure I write about personal patterns and personal understandings. Denise explained that self-knowledge and awareness are necessary and basic requirements to leading a happier, fuller, healthier life.

When Pam and Barry mentioned this idea to me I realized I had the opportunity to clarify my own thoughts. I had already written material describing that the secret to forming successful relationships with other creatures is to understand *oneself* first before moving on to understand others—but I just did not feel I was managing to convey the importance of this message. I agree with Denise that self-awareness is the building block to both individual happiness and in being able to form positive, long-term relationships with others.

The moment Pam and Barry told me of Denise's suggestion to include PPs (Personal Patterns) and PUs (Personal Understandings) into my writings I knew I had the key to emphasizing the nature of these important issues. What could be a more fundamental starting point to improving relationships with others? When I awake in the morning the first thing I consider are PPs and PUs. I know Reign and Katie have disciplined themselves to think the same way. That's why we get along so well.

I really like the idea of recognizing our own PUs so that we can apply ourselves to improving interaction with other dogs. When thinking about PPs I realized that most of us have patterns within our personalities where we become almost predictable in the things we do or the way we react in certain situations. If this is true I wondered if it is possible to change our less desirable patterns so that we can improve ourselves. It seems odd to me that most of us have the ability to recognize patterns in others, yet many of us struggle to see patterns within ourselves.

Can we change old habits? This question has been around a long time, as evidenced in the Bible (King James's version), where the question is posed: "Can an Ethiopian change his skin, or a leopard his spots?" I talked to Barry about this subject and asked him if, in reality, any of us could change our PPs. He was positive that we could, but he admitted that "unlearning" old and negative PPs could sometimes be very difficult. First, we must recognize a problem to be able to resolve it. Second, and just as importantly, it is imperative we have both the desire and a strong commitment to change.

My thinking is that if we want to change our PPs then we will need to have a clear set of PUs that will provide us with the insight on areas we will need to change. Understanding our own PPs is an essential step to moving forward. Only once we acknowledge the bad PPs (for example, the odiferous ones) that cause problems for ourselves and/or others can we move forward to the next step on the road toward successful interactions with our fellow beings.

We often repeat actions that might be offensive without even knowing we are doing so. It could be the way we react to events, perhaps it's an inflection in our bark, our whine, or our inability to empathize with others. Yet we repeat these actions and wonder why some folks do not respond well to us. It's kind of insane really. Confirmation of Einstein's theory on insanity.

How do we get a better understanding of our PPs?

One way is to face up to those PPs we know we should not have. Most of us know some of our "bad" PPs, but it takes character, effort, and desire to be better and to admit these faults to ourselves. We must learn to "self-observe." If you find that you are not getting a positive reaction from someone, try to analyze the situation from the other person's perspective. I believe many of us instinctively know the reason or cause for the poor reaction by others, but we most likely will try to put the blame elsewhere, since this is the easier path to take.

Barry often tells the tale of when he started to report to a new manager whose style was very different from his previous manager. His former boss wanted to be kept advised of any major developments but left the day-to-day operations for Barry to handle. The new guy wanted to know everything. At first, Barry resented what he termed the "micro-managing" of the business. After all, Barry had successfully run his operations for a number of years. Explaining every move to his new boss seemed to add no value and was an unnecessary encumbrance to the business. His boss was adamant, though, that he wanted to be told about everything. Soon communication problems started between them.

The situation looked set to deteriorate in an uncontrolled manner, so Barry decided to sit down and review what was going on. From his point of view, this "micro-managing" was insulting to him, and an unnecessary waste of time and money. But things were getting worse—with no solution in sight. Barry was getting shorter with his replies and his boss was becoming more insistent he be told every detail. Each conversation was leaving blood on the walls. Barry was quick to recognize, however, that the *only* blood on the walls was his! Barry's PP was to perform actions in his operation without having to explain his reasoning or actions to someone else.

It seemed that Barry would have to have a closer look into his PU. Why was his reaction so poor to this guy? After all, his new boss, despite his strong personality, was extremely likeable. It was hard to admit but Barry resented someone looking over his shoulder, he did not always react well to being scrutinized, and he certainly did not appreciate having to explain his decisions to others. Why? Was it through a fear of being wrong? Was his concern that he would be criticized? Barry never did respond well to criticism (he still doesn't, by the way, but at least now he understands it is one of his limitations). Was it because he thought he would lose control? Was it an issue of pride? Was Barry just being a stubborn SOD (Silly Old Dog)? The conclusion? Probably all of the above.

Something had to change. Why did this guy need all this information? Upon consideration, Barry decided that if he were just coming into the job as a complete outsider (his previous boss had been promoted to his position from within the company so already understood how things worked) he would want to learn the business in order to make the best decisions possible. Could this be the reason? If the guy was just a control freak then it was probably time for Barry to either just accept that (which was not something he wanted to live with) or move on. First, however, why not try a different tack? In other words, Barry would try to change his PP.

Unbidden, Barry started to send a brief DRO (Daily Report on Operations) to his manager. If there was news that Barry felt was of particular relevance to the business he picked up the telephone and called his superior. At first the response was a little muted, but slowly these reports and conversations became the focal point of the relationship. The two discussed items and his boss started to ask questions as to why Barry thought some items received priority or how they affected the business. Communications were cordial and friendly.

His boss was a quick learner, and Barry found their interactions stimulating because it forced him to take a look at certain parts of the operation with an eye to adding improvements. Within a short period of time his boss was satisfied he understood much more about the running of the business and told Barry his daily reports were no longer necessary; Barry should just call whenever something occurred that they should discuss. A bond of mutual trust was formed—and a lasting friendship. Barry discovered he really liked this gentleman and that he was an intelligent guy with strong business "smarts."

His boss's micro-managing was simply a reaction to wanting to learn the business. Other managers who wanted to prevent his boss from receiving that understanding would soon be gone. Of course, not all situations work out as positively as this one, but before jumping from the "frying pan into the fire" because of personal pride or because PPs direct your actions, try thinking if a change in approach might be warranted. In other words, don't be afraid to take a PP break.

Another method of reviewing PPs is to check with others to see how you are viewed and to ask them for suggestions for improvements. Performance reviews can often provide a source of information if approached positively. Of course, if your PP is to reject any inputs or thinking from others then this avenue of exploration will be closed to you.

A friend of Barry's once commented that he used to dread performance reviews, and heroically defended all observations about his character or work, automatically rejecting all suggestions for improvements. Needless to say, most reviewers used to write negative comments about his defensive reaction, and this counted against him regarding his leadership skills. Finally, he accepted that he should take note of what the reviewer was trying to tell him and vowed to improve himself in this area. It wasn't that long before he became the manager of his group. True leaders learn to learn by listening and accepting good ideas and suggestions.

Since I believe this to be true, that makes dogs the best leaders in the entire universe. As Robert Brault (author of *Round Up The Usual Subjects: Thoughts On Just About Everything*) once said: "If animals could talk, the world would lose its best listeners." Barry might disagree with Robert on this one since he complains bitterly that I am not listening to him when I'm out in the backyard on my own enjoying a good run around. Poor Barry, he totally fails to understand the difference between when someone is not listening to him and when they are choosing to ignore him.

Sometimes less desirable PPs can be taught inadvertently or on purpose by others. As young pups, for example, we tend to learn from the example of our elders. Try to be aware of this fact and question yourself to ensure the behavior you are being taught is personally and socially acceptable. I've always believed that instinctively most of us can recognize right from wrong on the major PPs. My advice to all young puppies is not to blindly copy other dogs. I also advise them that as they grow into adulthood they should not try to force their own style or actions onto others. While they may not mean harm, what might be right for one may not be right for someone else. Once the puppies have learned how to recognize some of their PPs, I counsel them not to be afraid of examining and questioning whether those PPs are appropriate for their chosen paths. Guard dogs may need to have aggression as part of their PPs—but this is not an appropriate trait for a therapy dog whose only desire is help humans feel better!

Here is an example of how poor behavior may be taught inadvertently and lead to a socially undesirable PP: I know several dog trainers who become frustrated when their students offer treats out of embarrassment to try to stop an animal from behaving badly. By offering rewards this way the student is actually reinforcing the very thing he or she is trying to stop. By rewarding good behavior, it is possible to prevent bad behavior. Be careful not to confuse accidentally rewarding bad behavior with deliberately rewarding good.

To illustrate this let me tell you a little story about our family's personal walking patterns. When out on a walk, should a runner come toward us too quickly, Reign and Katie will inevitably want to start barking and pulling on their leashes. Personally, if someone wants to tire themselves out by running themselves into the ground then I think that's their hard luck. I just glance at the runner with a look of pity. Pam, being a very smart lady, will quickly take out one of our favorite treats as soon as a runner appears. Instantly, all of us will sit down and turn our attention toward those tasty little morsels. The runner normally passes by unnoticed, and we are given a little snack. If we do see a runner, walker, or something else coming to invade our space when we are with Pam, we immediately think "treat time" and ready ourselves accordingly.

Barry, on the other hand, usually forgets to take treats with him. He lives in a world of his own most of the time so does not even see the runner coming. Reign and Katie are keen to protect Barry, even though the only person he really needs protection from is himself. As the runner approaches, my girls form an army of two to defeat the oncoming foe. Barry shouts a lot and pulls on the leads, but frankly he's fighting a losing battle. Sometimes I join in just for the fun of it. His attempts at controlling three 50lb-plus, strong, athletic dogs are hilarious—but the girls and I get a real kick out of seeing him try! Pam constantly has to tell Barry to put treats in his pocket when he takes us for a walk, but she is fighting a losing battle most of the time, too. It's such a shame!

I have listened to many discussions that my companions have had with others—and it appears that most humans are very happy to talk about, and point out, weaknesses in others, but few take criticism of themselves well. Of course, the timing and the way the observation is delivered is extremely important as to whether the criticism feels positive and fair to the individual on the receiving end. When trying to "help" someone, ask yourself how you would feel if the remarks were made to you at that time and in that fashion. Often well-meaning pointers for improvement will be taken poorly, and I have even seen friendships break up as a result of a criticism that was delivered at the wrong time or in the wrong way. I well remember Reign making an aggressive comment to me about getting near her food one day. I sulked for two days and growled at her for about a week if she so much as pointed her paw in the direction of *my* bowl.

Barry told me that many companies spend a great deal of money and time in an effort to select the right people for the right job. Personality profiling—sometimes referred to as psychometric testing or psychological profiling testing—is often used to determine whether a candidate's personality will suit the function for which they have applied. Some groups, apparently, use personality profiling to provide insights into how an individual's performance can be improved through selective mentoring or training.

We dogs profile other dogs through the traditional tried-and-true method of bottom sniffing. You can learn so much about another dog this way! Why is this convention frowned upon in the human world? Why this should be deemed unacceptable seems odd to me. How do you ever discover anything about each other if you cannot sniff each other's private parts?

Humans, it seems, prefer to rely on impressions and instinct (which, as we shall establish later on, they don't know how to use properly). I asked Barry if there were ways that your species could find to learn more about yourselves and others in order to take some of the guesswork out of relationships. He told me there were.

Enlightened companies, it seems, often offer training with personal assessment tools that can be used to improve work productivity, teamwork, and communication. There are a variety of different personal assessment tools available. I will select just one to use here: the DiSC® program. It is my understanding that the majority of other assessment tools use similar principles.

DiSC® is a commercially available assessment tool based on the DISC theory of psychologist William Moulton Marston. Marston's work identified and centered on four different personality traits: Dominance, Inducement, Submission, and Compliance. The DiSC® program is geared toward providing insights to an individual's PUs and PPs and those of other people. In this program, the acronym DiSC® stands for Dominance, Influence, Steadiness, and Conscientiousness. There are many assessment tools available today that can easily be found using the internet. You simply need to choose the one that seems to be the best fit for your own objectives.

Barry has taken the DiSC® training several times and introduced it into many of the groups he managed in order to help employee personal career development. Answering the detailed questionnaire at the beginning of the program leads to a personality profile graph. One day, Barry dropped all of his personal DiSC® course papers on the floor—so I took time out to paw over them to see what all the fuss was about. I also took a peak at Barry's profile—and the results were really something to bark about!!! It certainly gave me insight as to why he acts the way he does sometimes.

It is extremely important to clearly understand that these personal assessment tools are non-judgmental! In other words, as you find yourself falling into a certain type of behavior pattern or profile (PP), the intention is only to help you recognize where you and others are by using a common language. No profile is better, or worse, than any other. Recognizing your own PP, as well as that of others, will allow you to understand, appreciate, and communicate far more effectively with others. It will also help you to develop skills for your chosen career path as you move forward. The world needs different types of personalities and skills to function properly. If everyone was the same then we would be in chaos! Imagine if all of us were profiled as being exceptionally high Ds. We would all be characterized as "Dominant"—and the dog versus dog world war would probably break out immediately!

Consider the following to illustrate what I mean by the world needing different capabilities and skills: Certain breeds of dogs have skills that have been developed over time in order for them to be the best at what they need to do. For example, a bloodhound would not win a speed race against a greyhound. On the other hand, a bloodhound has an amazing sense of smell and can find things that few other dogs can detect. How many people do you know who are capable of following a scent and finding a cadaver in water like the bloodhound?

To really appreciate the talents of we beautifully sculptured canines, look at how many police forces use dogs. In the United States, we are known as the "K-9" section. I love that name. It's so apt, don't you think? We are used as enforcement or guard dogs, to find illicit substances or to discover explosives, for SAR (Search And Rescue), tracking, crowd control, cases of arson, and even to find bodies of deceased people (that one is bit of a dead-end job in my opinion). I've heard some amazing stories of how dogs have dedicated themselves to a task in order to help their human friends.

Humans are also multi-faceted beings. You sometimes don't

recognize this about yourselves, and this is where assessment tools can really help. Once you understand more about yourself and your abilities and can acknowledge the personality traits and skills of others, you will have a greater appreciation of how to communicate and take advantage of similarities and differences amongst each other.

Discovering how you can improve your own skills by relating to others can be satisfying and rewarding. As John Ray noted in his *Collection of English Proverbs* in 1678: *"It's the nature o' th' beast."* To me this means that, even unconsciously, every creature has certain characteristic traits. To know and understand these traits, and to use that understanding to work better and more effectively with your fellow man, not only provides a more fun and harmonious working environment, but surely is also an excellent step in knowing how to become a manager of people. Some individuals are good managers of their businesses, some are visionaries and can lead by example, but not all are necessarily good *people* managers. It seems to me that those who can combine all of these skills can aspire to become great leaders and captains of industry.

You can take the DiSC® assessments on-line and self-score. Reading about each type of profile will give you an idea of your personality traits, strengths, and possible weaknesses as they relate to others. Pay attention to all of the profile factors so you can understand people who have differing characteristics. I've heard Barry say he always enjoyed working through these tests under the tutelage of an expert with other students present. This gave him the opportunity to compare and discuss results. Further, the group was able to see how accurately they could recognize each other's profiles. That sounds like fun!

Barry told me the DiSC® training helped him in his selling roles since he was able to better assess customers and their potential requirements. For example, Barry knew that trying to sell detailed specifications of the performance of a product to a "High D" (High Ds like to think about the big picture rather than fuss over details) may be a waste of time. A High D, however, is likely to be impressed if, in a few words, a product can be shown to add value to his company's overall performance. High Ss or Cs are likely to demand proof, and to research into the matter in some detail before simply accepting a claim from a seller of the product. High Is, on the other hand, will probably want to hold a meeting to socialize any decision. Which of the profiles will make the best decision? All of them, in their own way, depending on circumstances. In reality, of course, most people have a spread of personality traits in their makeup, so sometimes determining the exact profile of another can take some skill and be quite challenging.

Being the intelligent soul that I am I decided to develop my own canine assessment program in order to help myself and my fellow furry friends develop a closer relationship with their human partners. The program, which I have called BaRC™, essentially operates in a similar way to DiSC®. The groups within BaRC™ are: Brave, Assertive, Respectful, and Cuddly.

As with DiSC®, dogs are asked to respond to statements and then give answers with a bark, yelp, growl, whine, or howl to see how strongly they agree, or disagree, with the statements. For example, one question asks dogs to respond to the statement: "My human companion thinks I can be too aggressive about my ownership of a bone." The dog can choose to "strongly agree" (loud bark), "agree" (high-pitched yelp), "neutral" (deep growl), "disagree" (annoying whine), or "strongly disagree" (ear-piercing howl). Upon completion of the questionnaire, the scores for each category are added and assigned to the personality graph. Are you surprised to learn that we Vizslas score well in all categories—since, of course, we are such brave, friendly, cuddly, modest, and brilliant animals at all things we do! But, as I said, this is not a competition and the program is non-judgmental. It's simply a fact, though, that we Vizslas do well at so many things.

My D.E.V is that understanding more about yourself and others will make for a much happier working environment. It will make the challenge of working with and through others a much easier task and lead to an increase in your respect for the abilities of others whilst engendering respect for you from those around you. Further, it will yield improved results from both inside and outside of the company and be a good step toward learning how to manage people if that is a direction you would like to take. If you are prepared to accept and understand that differences among people are actually good and necessary for the company to function properly, then you will be pleasantly surprised at just how easy it is to have a positive relationship with those that you may not have had much respect for in the past. As you learn more about how others contribute to the well-being of the company, you will find that just because some tasks may not be as glamourous as others, without someone willing to perform them, and perform them well, the company and its reputation will decline.

Understanding that everyone has value is important. As an illustration, think about your own reaction as a customer when you deal with companies that do not respond well should issues arise. Perhaps you have placed an order that arrived damaged in transit. You wanted to buy the product because the company had an excellent advertisement on television. When you called the sales number to inquire about the product, the sales person was warm, friendly, and very helpful. You were given all the information you needed to purchase and placing and paying for the order was a simple task. But the parcel arrived damaged because it was packed badly. When you called to complain, the person you talked to was difficult, refused to accept that the package had arrived in a damaged condition—and tried to convince you that somehow the damage was your fault!

Even if the issue is fully resolved to your complete satisfaction—would you really want to buy from that company again? And how many people will you tell about your experience with that company? (I'll give you some answers to those questions in a later Thought!) The company will have spent a huge amount of money designing, manufacturing, and promoting their products. The company has trained their sales staff at great expense, with systems in place to handle customer orders and billing quickly and efficiently. Yet they could fail because their shipping department just does not care? Oh yes, everyone in the company matters!

From this handsome and cuddly canine's point of view, I know that not every dog can look as beautiful as me. Some are small, some are hairy, and, in my view, some are just plain ugly. Yet I respect them all because they do jobs that I just am unable or unwilling to do. As an added bone-us (sorry, couldn't resist that one!) I have an extended range of friends where we all respect one another. Playtime is just a bark away!

THOUGHT THREE

Barking Mad
~*Communications*

Interpersonal communications for humans seem to provide some real problems. Dogs are so much better at figuring out who they want to be with or who will not fit well into their world. As previously mentioned: Dogs sniff each other to establish credentials. After a few sniffs we use our natural instincts to decide how to go forward with any strangers. We either get tough—we growl, bark, or gnash our teeth—or we choose to wag our tails and ask our new chum if they would like to play.

We can often tell at first smell if we want to be friends with, or murder, any strangers. You guys touch each other with your hands, retreat quickly, and say "err" a lot. You don't even take a quick close-up whiff of each other—so how the heck you can ever figure out if the other person is foe or friend is beyond my ken. It was Charles Darwin who once wisely said: "Man himself cannot express love and humility by external signs, so plainly as does a dog, when with drooping ears, hanging lips, flexuous body, and wagging tail, he meets his beloved master."

Somebody called Anonymous proclaimed: "If your dog doesn't like someone you probably shouldn't either." I agree with Anon.

You clearly do not understand your own ability to act on your instincts, either, because I cannot tell you how many times I've heard some idiot exclaim, "I should never have got involved with the guy. I could see he was bad, I could smell it a mile off," only to relate how they had suffered at the hands of this individual. You can see and smell, but you fail to take any notice of your instincts! You would not last five minutes in our world.

Animals communicate with each other through sounds, body language, touch, taste, smell, and even silence (which for some species can signify danger). Not true for humans, who nowadays have a wonderful way of avoiding any of these types of communications with each other through the use of something labeled "technology."

By typing messages into boxes called smartphones, tablets, or computers, you don't have to see, hear, touch, or smell another human—and yet you can still "communicate" with each other! Listening to your conversations when you do finally get together, however, suggests to me that communicating through the use of technology can sometimes be risky at best.

I have often heard someone say that they completely misunderstood another's electronic message and it was only later by talking directly to the individual that the misunderstandings were sorted out.

My observation here is that electronic communication is wonderful for keeping in touch with others, confirming conversations, as a means of keeping records, providing information, or for setting up appointments. Computers can also be used for conveying thoughts to a wider audience—as I am doing by writing this book. But electronic messaging should not replace more personal means (such as face-to-face or ear-to-ear discussions) to resolve issues where understanding another's point of view is important.

Never use the electronic media to relieve yourself of anger. You may have "stewed" over a certain subject, and then decided to "clear the air" by writing about all the points that have offended you. A very dangerous practice indeed! If you insist on sending a clear message this way, my advice is: Send your note to the "draft" file, sit on it for an hour or two (or better still, overnight) and, once you have cooled down a little, reread it before pressing the "send" button. You will be surprised at how often you will be glad you operated this way.

Barry told me he always tried to do this as part of his SOP (Standard Operating Procedure, but I think it should stand for Silly Old Person), and, on many occasions, he was grateful he did. He said he was sometimes horrified by how he could include some very offensive and unnecessary put downs into his original messages. By rewriting his notes, he could still manage to get his points across but avoid hurtful and pointless comments.

The best communication method is to hear and see what someone has to say—even if it's later transferred electronically to confirm the conversation. Voice inflection and body language can tell you a great deal about the real message being delivered. I can assure you that when another dog's hackles rise and he starts growling at me in a deep, throaty way I back off pretty quickly—as he is telling me he is really upset with me. I may not always understand the reason and will probably check in later to see if I'm continuing to cause offense. The initial body and voice language, however, told me all I needed to understand in order for me to avoid getting hurt.

Barry often cites the management training videos offered by a company called Video Arts in the United Kingdom. Many of the early videos starred John Cleese of Monty Python fame. The "How Not to Do It" example is shown first, and then the correct method is subsequently screened.

Barry loves these training films and reckons he can name managers with whom he was acquainted who embraced the "How Not to Do It" strategy. The initial scenes are hilarious, often seemingly bizarre and farfetched, yet most people can cite examples of their own where they have witnessed managers acting in the way depicted. While face-to-face meetings don't necessarily solve every problem, nonetheless there are always situations when an in-person conversation, a video chat, or even a phone call are better choices than sending e-mail messages to one another.

Barry tells of the time when two managers were sending e-mails to one another and he was being cc'd, or copied, on their correspondence. The e-mail exchange was heating up between the two when, finally,

Barry could stand it no longer. He left his desk and strode down the corridor and into the office of the two individuals concerned. "Why don't you two just talk to one another directly, especially as your desks face each other? And stop involving me on an issue you can resolve between you in a couple of minutes!" he blazed. Both managers looked up at him in astonishment. Neither had apparently considered this option. They had simply fallen into the trap of sending e-mails out on everything they did—and yes, the issue was resolved in very short order and all parties ended up seeing the funny side of the story.

Years ago, Barry received an e-mail that appeared to leave him out of a senior management meeting to which he had expected an invitation. He expressed surprise to his manager who reviewed the message, grunted, and said, "It's not very clear. Never assume against yourself. Give the sender a call to clarify." Barry did, and the originator of the message was truly taken aback that his note seemed to indicate anything else other than an invite—until he re-read it for himself. The sender apologized profusely for his unclear message and immediately sent out a proper invitation.

Barry was working for his mentor and friend, Juergen, at the time of this incident. Juergen had an amazing ability to state deep and meaningful phrases that contained a unique philosophy of life. The phrase, "Never assume against yourself," became famous throughout the company. To this day, our companions, especially in their private lives, apply this saying when communications with others are less than clear. It is truly astounding how many times Pam and Barry have used this philosophy, even regarding family matters, and, as a result, situations that could easily have spiraled out of control have been avoided.

Animals cannot communicate through texting, e-mailing, or social media—and therefore misunderstandings of this type are unknown. You might want to consider this fact when sending or receiving messages. If someone sends an e-mail, says something, or even quotes something another person has said, where the meaning is unclear, avoid taking it to mean that it is intended to offend in some way. Check it out. You will always be glad you did. Most times, the individual you have identified as an offender will be surprised or taken aback at the slant you have put on their comment. On the other hand, if they did mean something negative you will know exactly where you stand.

I have one other thought for you to consider before I close on this subject. When I pawed through the definition of "communication," I was surprised to find so many variances in the explanations. The more complex the explanation, the more wide-ranging the subject. But there was one definition that really struck home with me: "The imparting or exchanging of information or news."

Imparting or exchanging of information seemed fairly straightforward to me, although the way this can happen is exceptionally broad! Still, the word "news" in the definition really intrigued me.

How do companies generally impart news? We all know that good news spreads quickly and easily, and most companies are usually pretty good at letting employees know when good news abounds. Unfortunately, bad news, whether real or perceived, spreads even quicker. Bad news can do a great deal of damage if left unchecked or uncorrected.

For reasons we dogs cannot fathom, humans seem to feel it's better to hide bad news from their companions. This can only lead to misunderstandings and loss of trust. And no news is the worst kind of news of all. Animals just don't do this to each other—so why do you?

Employees will start to generate their own ideas when a company or manager tries to brush unpleasant information under the carpet. First, employees are more aware of, or have an instinct for, when things are not going well. There is an intelligence system within an organization that sends up warning signals at the first hint of trouble. Second, most managers don't impart bad news because they fear that employees' morale will be damaged. Actually, most employees have a resilience that will surprise you. The majority of people deal with some sort of bad news every day. Most people know how to handle bad news—although it's true that many don't know how to handle the lack of information well. Employees would much rather be told the truth than have the fear that management is hiding things from them.

We animals openly share bad news—no matter how much it hurts and no matter how much it feels like admitting defeat. Usually we make a lot of noise about it, too. I have no hesitation in sharing the bad news with my companions that my bowls have no food or water. I'm normally pretty vociferous about it—as they can testify!

Employees will respect you for sharing. Barry told me that often employees put forward suggestions to help resolve problems he and his managers may not have considered palatable to the workforce. As discussed elsewhere in this book, we tend to make assumptions on behalf of others about what they want or how they are motivated. All too often the assumptions are only partially true or just flat wrong. Usually employees are anxious to share the pain and help in any way they can. The majority of employees have a need to feel involved in the company, and management should encourage that involvement—for with involvement comes ownership. With ownership comes commitment. With commitment comes success.

Barry recalled one instance when his group was doing pretty well, but elsewhere the company was having a hard time. The requirement for a RIF (Reduction in Force) had been issued from corporate. Discussions with senior management about killing the goose that laid the golden egg, and so on, yielded no result—and the message was clear: Reduce headcount by 5 percent with people and positions of the teams' choice—or corporate would send their own people to do the job. Corporate was offering a generous termination package to soften the blow.

Barry talked through the situation with his direct reports and asked each department manager to perform a critical review of resources. It was a case of trying to eliminate positions that would do the least amount of damage to the teams' overall performance. These are heart-rending exercises, so Barry tried not to pressure managers—but at the same time he remained firm.

A list of positions and people was put together. Not wishing to simply issue an ultimatum, Barry called a companywide meeting to explain what was going on, what the requirements from corporate were, and the timing of the actions to be taken. These meetings are miserable occasions at best, but Barry had discovered many years before that people could handle bad news—they just could not handle lack of news. Some other groups in the company just handed out dismissal notices and left HR to explain the termination packages to the affected employees.

To his amazement (and pride in the people who worked for the company) three members of the staff stood up and volunteered to take the package and leave the company. Two said they had been contemplating retirement and felt it was important to step aside in order to protect the younger and more vulnerable members of the community. These were seasoned veterans and some of the very last individuals that the managers would have chosen. Selecting someone close to retirement is usually seen by the victim's co-workers as convenient for the company—but nonetheless heartless and mean. Since these folks had stepped up to the plate for themselves they were regarded by their co-workers with respect. Had the company chosen the same people the workforce would have regarded them as victims of company "policy." The other volunteer admitted he had just been told his mother, who lived far away, was terminally ill and had less than a year to live. He had been struggling with the decision as to whether to leave the company and move to look after his mother or stay and keep the job he enjoyed so much. He felt grateful that the company had made his agonizing choice much easier, and the termination package would help him financially.

An interesting conclusion to this story: A couple of years later, when the good times returned and the company had grown, this last gentleman came back and rejoined the company in a slightly higher position than when he had left. His mother had died after 18 months, and it had taken another nine months for him to conclude all her affairs and move back to Tennessee. He had completed several courses to improve his education during his period away from the company. He remains one of the company's most loyal, hardworking, and dedicated employees.

Ultimately, it was the employees of each department, working with their supervisors, who provided the final list. The terminations were completed, and, as much as anything can be in a situation like this, everyone was satisfied with the result. It goes without saying that Barry was extremely fortunate and very rarely will things work out as they did in this case, but for me the message was clear: Share news, good or bad, and be prepared to listen. In the animal kingdom we share information and news all the time. And believe me: Bad news travels fast! If it didn't many of us would not be here to tell the tale (or even wag our tail).

My D.E.V. in this area is that quality communication with others is extremely important as a way to foster successful relationships and create healthy business practices. Don't ignore your instincts, and don't be afraid to be open to others. Use technology to communicate, but don't let technology substitute for good old-fashioned human-to-human contact.

Be open in your communications. Share good news, of course, but be prepared to let everyone know the bad news, too. Sharing factual news, good or bad, is actually a positive thing to do, but spreading unsubstantiated information or conjecture is simply gossip and rumor mongering.

Supervisors and managers should realize that employees deserve to be treated with respect, and when you share news you are showing respect. In turn, employees will respect you for sharing. Trying to hide information or trying to gloss over items that seem less than positive causes suspicion and distrust. During the harder times, most employees will want to make a contribution toward improving company performance.

Quality communications can avoid employees fighting among themselves because of a lack of trust in the management or company—or, as I term it, falling victim to the "dog-eat-dog" syndrome.

Thought Four

'bout Time for a Treat
~ *Expectations*

What have I learned about rewards as I have matured? Expect nothing. Demand even less. Hope for everything. Trust in your God (even though She might be a Great Dane—not that I have anything against Great Danes, but you must admit they are *big*). And: Take every action possible to make your dreams a reality.

How did I learn this lesson? I loved treats as a young pup. I was given treats for performing tricks, for doing as I was bid—and for just looking irresistibly cute (that last one was very easy!). Even I have to admit I soon had "cute" down to a fine art. Most humans are as soft as warm butter—and good things always came my way when I turned on my irresistible charm and simply looked as beautiful as I naturally am. As my puppyhood progressed I became less inclined to work for a treat as a reward, and I began to think of treats as my right. After all, I allowed my human companions to love on me—and in return I cuddled up to them and gave them comfort!

I started to demand treats by not doing as I was told until I had received my rightful reward. Pam began talking about the dreadful teens, but I have no idea what she meant by that. Pam and Barry became irritated by what I was doing, but what were they going to do—stop loving the most wonderful canine on the planet? Uh-uh—not gonna happen! Then, suddenly, just like that, they stopped giving me treats—and started taking me instead for training lessons! I was horrified!

At first the lessons were difficult. I did not understand why Pam and Barry were doing this to me or what they expected of me. I tried to play with the other dogs, but they would not even let me do this. The trainer, Paula, who became a good friend of ours and eventually partner to Pam in her animal therapy and massage business, started by explaining that the biggest cause of my "problem" was with my human companions, rather than with me. I could have explained that to them right off the bat! After all, it was Pam and Barry who had stopped giving my rightful treats. What was so difficult to understand about that?

Paula went on to explain the steps she would take to make the world a safer place for me and to allow Pam and Barry to have more authority with me. This way my companions would be more in charge. I almost stuck my paw down my throat! Humans "in charge"? What a notion! Looking back, though, I have to confess: The classes were great fun, and I really looked forward to attending them. I also received many treats when I performed to the trainer's satisfaction. Most enjoyable. I particularly enjoyed the "socialization" part of the training, as I made a number of new friends with whom I was allowed to play at the beginning and end of the sessions.

I quickly discovered when we returned home that I was only going to earn treats for being obedient and not for misbehaving. For those members of my species that will become irate at being treated this way (no pun intended), I would say: "Peace." The act of working together with my humans actually brought us closer together as a family. I was allowed more freedom to do what I wanted, my companions were far more relaxed, loving times were extended, and I was on the receiving end of a host of treats.

Barry told me that many people believe being employed by someone is their "right," but, in reality, everyone who has a job should be thankful for the privilege. I know: Some companies do not treat their employees with respect, some managers fail to understand the benefits of having good employees, and even colleagues do not always recognize how to work effectively alongside of their fellow beings. But I do know there are no "rights" to employment (although you guys do have rights once you are employed!), as many can testify who have worked hard and still lost their jobs through no fault of their own. I do know, though, that a positive attitude toward work benefits everyone.

I understand that working conditions can often be the cause of negativity. Poor management, perceived unfairness, unsatisfactory monetary valuation for a position, poor communication, or even changes caused by reorganizations can be unsettling and undermine confidence. Always consider, however, that rarely are positive results created from negative responses. As I always say: A wagging tail is worth a thousand whines!

Many corporations talk the talk about wanting employees to be bold in their actions and to not be afraid to make mistakes as they move forward, yet when things go wrong many times corporate managers are swift with their retribution, even if the reason is beyond the control of the employee. Often when blame needs to be apportioned as a way to deflect corporate ire away from the manager involved, someone is chosen as being responsible for the mistake. The victim is often referred to as a "scapegoat." I assume this individual must be good at producing milk or cheese.

Try to always create a positive result from a bad situation. If you regard every mistake made, no matter who makes it, as an opportunity to learn and improve, I promise that good things will happen—and morale within the workforce will elevate.

Barry often tells a story about a salesman (we will call him Dan, although this is not his real name) who worked for a large corporation. Dan lost an important sale involving millions of dollars—and knew he was in deep trouble. Dan had overpromised to a client on a delivery date to try to sweeten a deal, but the customer had become aware this date could not be met. The bond of trust was severed by this one misleading promise. Dan was called into his CEO's office for a discussion. Before Dan left for his "visit" to the CEO's office he packed up his personal belongings. Dan knew when someone was fired, a security guard was called to clean out the desk of the miscreant and hand him his belongings on his way out the door.

Just as an aside, did you know that being "fired" has a different meaning to being "sacked?" In olden times, craftsmen used to carry their tools in a sack from job to job. When the project was complete, or the services of the craftsman were no longer required (I suppose the modern equivalent is a "lay-off"), the sack of tools was returned to the craftsman to signify the end. If the craftsman caused an offence (such as being violent or stealing), the sack of tools was burned (or "fired"). Without his tools the craftsman would have difficulty being re-employed.

Back to the main story: Dan entered the CEO's office and was met with the grim face of his corporate master. The CEO told Dan he would only ask one question and urged Dan to give him a truthful and sincere answer. The question posed was: "What, if anything, did you learn from this experience?" Dan had pondered this for himself, so his answer came to him easily. "Never betray the trust of the customer simply to get the sale," he said, and he headed toward the door. "Where do you think you are going?" inquired the CEO. Dan said that he was going home to refresh his resume and to start applying for a new job. The CEO stared at him. "Why?" he asked. "Because I have been fired, and my family and I need to eat," replied the disconsolate Dan. The CEO laughed and looked Dan squarely in the eyes. "I have just invested several millions of dollars in you so you could learn a valuable lesson. Why the merry dickens would I fire you?"

Dan went on to be one of the best, highest-producing, and most loyal employees in the company's history. You see: That CEO was a true leader and understood the value of lessons well learned.

I have learned that it is the way you react to resolving issues after mistakes are made that will determine the ultimate outcome of the error. Companies that accept mistakes as an opportunity to improve, that step up to the plate and are honest with their customers by recognizing any problems, and then resolve issues to the satisfaction of the customer, are those that succeed in the long run. As good old Confucius used to say, "Our greatest glory is not in never falling, but in rising every time we fall."

If I make a "mistake," such as chewing up the newspaper, by far and away the best way for me to handle the situation is to apologize profusely to my human companions, take full responsibility for my actions, and run straight to my crate. I then look totally crestfallen, heartbroken even, by my misdeed, and slump miserably to the floor with my paws over my head to show contrition. It is no accident that I look really cute in this position, and I am fully aware that Pam and Barry will often turn away from me to hide their laughter at my look of utter despair and misery. I hope I have offered some helpful hints on how to deal with irate customers!

Recently, Pam was reading an article about training a dog by using "operant behavior." If I understand the theory correctly, the idea is to let a dog learn by discovery, because in the wild this is how puppies learn to survive. Once the puppy makes a discovery, he or she receives a reward, such as a treat or playtime with the trainer. When these "accidents" (discoveries) occur, then the act itself is imprinted on the animal's mind and is a lesson learned forever.

Pam was amazed when she clicked on the video that accompanied the article. The trainer took an untrained puppy and literally within minutes had it performing a perfect recall. No anger, no yelling, no irritation—just fun and rewards for everyone. The art of training the puppy to continue to learn what the trainer wanted was to plan ahead in such a way that the "accidents" became a natural part of the program.

The trainer went on to say that, unfortunately for humans, dogs also "condition" their owners as well. Dogs often learn that if they want something and they pester their companions sufficiently, eventually the reward will come. I have seen many human children doing the same thing to their parents, so why it took a dog trainer to "discover" this secret is beyond my comprehension.

Barry thinks many of the lessons learned from dog training can apply to the workplace, too. He told me that, in his view, encouraging employees to discover things for themselves through their mistakes is a healthy practice. I have observed that most strong leaders act this way. We will talk more about this in a later chapter, but I believe the point Barry is trying to make is that managers can plan ahead to allow some "accidents" to happen (or at least not step in to stop mistakes being made) since the lessons learned are carried with the employee throughout their career. Encouraging people to not be afraid of failure, but rather to be afraid of not trying, will bring benefits as well. As Michael Jordan once said, "I can accept failure, everyone fails at something. But I can't accept not trying."

Rewarding employees for achievements makes sense, too, because employees will be eager to please if their efforts are recognized. Even verbal recognition from a company, manager, or colleague can be very powerful for most people. Saying "good job" really does matter! I love it when Pam or Barry say, "Good Boy!" even when I don't receive a treat. When one of my companions understands that I have acted in a positive fashion and offers me praise, my tail just waves uncontrollably in the air to show my pleasure. Being recognized is fun!

Unfortunately, there are some employees who learn how to "condition" their employer or supervisor. These employees become so upset or abusive when something happens not to their liking that their manager or supervisor begins to fear them. Such troublesome employees often ensure that management retribution or reprisal never occurs because the company fears having to deal with the "hothead." Regrettably, if actions are not taken against such agitators, a negative message is sent to other, less demanding workers: That it pays to be a troublemaker.

I am certainly not saying people in the workforce should avoid standing up for themselves. There are those, however, who simply love to cause trouble for the sake of causing trouble. If a pack animal consistently causes trouble do you know what happens? The pack will ostracize, ignore, or runoff the troublemaker!

You don't have to be a manager or in any senior position to have an effect; the key here is to simply not allow troublemakers to be indecorous. Most troublemakers will verbalize their intentions of "advising" management of their objections by outlining the intended approach to their friends and colleagues before doing anything. The troublemaker is usually looking to test any holes in their argument and is trying to garner support from those around. If you have doubts about what is to be said, you do not feel comfortable with the way the approach will be made, or you consider the issue not important enough to make a fuss over, make sure that the troublemaker is aware of your concerns. Most people tend to not say anything and the troublemaker will take this silence as agreement to their points. Let the troublemaker know you will not support them. If you disagree with the troublemaker tell them so.

Unfortunately, many times troublemakers are also bullies—and if you fail to take their side or agree with them they will turn their anger toward you. I have even seen one of these bullies threaten physical harm to someone who disagreed with them. In this particular case it was a German Shepherd who did not want to play ball with his companion. The other dog present, a Chihuahua, disagreed as he wanted so badly to play chase the ball. The Chihuahua made his position clear in a high-pitched voice to both his companion and the German Shepherd. The German Shepherd was clearly put out by his smaller colleague's failure to follow his lead and snapped his teeth as a warning to the Chihuahua. To the German Shepherd's amazement, the Chihuahua barked right into the Shepherd's face, causing the German Shepherd to leap back in alarm. The Chihuahua then disdainfully turned his back on the other dog and encouraged his companion to throw the ball. The German Shepherd just sat down, looking very perplexed and uncertain as to what he should do next.

My take from this episode is that you don't have to be big, or aggressive, to disagree with others. You are entitled to your thoughts and wishes. Equally, you should respect the fact that others are entitled to have a different opinion to your own.

A lack of discipline will cause problems for supervisors, other staff and, ultimately, the company. Most companies have rules or systems that have to be followed. I much prefer rules for only the most basic parts of the operation, supplemented by guidelines that offer a framework of expectations. Rigid systems can often be abused and can force a company to write more rules and regulations to correct the abuse.

It is impossible to foresee every issue that might arise, and extensive rules can mitigate a manager's flexibility in response to unusual circumstances. Ask employees to seek other employment if they abuse the trust placed in them. Some folks will never change—unless they learn that actions have consequences. If you have no authority over these individuals then my advice is to let them know of your disdain over their activities.

You don't have to be confrontational—just a simple comment to let them know of your disapproval often works. Barry often uses humor and says that taking "the Mickey" (which I believe refers to a large mouse who reportedly has many homes, including California and Florida) often has more effect on these troublesome characters than getting angry with them. I'm not completely convinced about this since sometimes I fear his humor flies over the miscreants' heads and they think he is offering a compliment.

Rules generally don't solve problems if someone is determined to use the system for their own perceived benefit. Ask any government employee in any country why they have so many rules—and they will tell you about their efforts to prevent wrongdoers from perpetrating and perpetuating system abuses. Ironically, when new rules are established in an attempt to prevent further misuse, it's normally those that have been honest in their efforts to operate within the system that end up being punished. I'm sure you all have examples of where this has happened.

Barry regularly whines about tax forms that become increasingly more complex with each passing year. Tax authorities try to prevent "abusers" from finding loopholes in the rules that they can use to their own advantage—but so often the offenders manage to find another hole. Sadly, a number of well-known corporations are very much a part of this activity. Some large companies employ people or other companies to seek out loopholes—usually under the guise of protecting shareholder value. Many times, the senior management forget to mention that they get paid handsome bonuses for this activity. Nothing will change as long as we all tolerate this type of behavior! I know Pam and Barry are quick to react if, for example, having said "no" to my licking their plates I try to find another way around the problem.

Barry tells me that most people feel unable to influence the behavior by large companies to circumnavigate the law (especially tax law). He did tell me, however, about a group of friends of ours who have "blacklisted" any companies that knowingly seek to take advantage of loop holes in the law. Our friends have standing instructions with their brokers not to invest any money in such companies. My immediate thought is that it will make little difference to the offending companies if a few people do not invest in their business. Then I began to consider that if more and more people took action by not investing in certain groups, the companies concerned may well eventually start to see a deterioration in the stock price. Now wouldn't that make the CEOs (and stockholders) of those companies sit up and take notice?

It may surprise you to know that a recent survey estimated that at least 10 percent of the S&P 500 companies (some of the largest corporations in the world) avoid paying U.S. taxes. There are lists of corporate tax dodgers to be found on the internet. Try looking them up. All of the corporations identified in these lists are household names and I, for one, thought the majority of them were reputable companies. Barry said he was not shocked, but then went off to sulk because one of them was his favorite mobile telephone company! I think he knows less than he lets on sometimes.

In my experience, if another creature sets out to cheat in some way on one issue, chances are they will usually lie or do wrong in other areas, too. I don't like having these characters around me. We animals have a saying: "One bad piece of meat can ruin the feast." My dogma, as you might say, is to have high expectations for my fellow beings. I provide them with clear guidelines, usually by curling up my lips to reveal my sparkling and outstanding fangs, when wrongdoing is about to happen. I overlay this with my philosophy on the subject matter through demonstrating how I would like things to be done.

In this way they understand the right way to handle things, and then

I trust them not to abuse my trust. If that trust is broken offenders are quickly removed from my life. I seldom lose my temper, but when I do most animals are sensible enough to realize that removing themselves from my presence is the healthy thing to do. It rarely comes to this, though, since most guys cotton on pretty fast and quickly depart of their own volition. I have to admit: My deep growl can be very intimidating.

The D.E.V. here: Understand that nothing in life is a given. There are no "rights" to employment. There should be no expectation that someone, somewhere, must look after you or that handouts should be available to anyone who demands or asks for them. In every society there are those who, for reasons beyond their control, are unable to make their way in the world without assistance. These individuals, creatures, or groups of people are those that we should all seek to help and protect. I strongly believe that we should provide for those less fortunate than ourselves. We animals are often part of a herd, pack, or some form of collective for that very reason; we seek to protect and look after one another—because, after all, one day it might be one of us who needs help.

Only the other day Pam was showing us a video of a herd of elephants that ran to provide assistance to an elephant calf that had become stuck in mud by the edge of a river. The calf was in danger of sinking into the quagmire and drowning. Within seconds the parents were on the scene in a desperate effort to free the calf but were unable to do so on their own. Shortly afterward other members of the herd arrived, and, working with each other, they slowly dragged the calf to the side of the river.

A heartwarming story indeed—but consider the facts: One member of the team was in trouble. Even the closest members were unable to provide an answer by themselves. With help from the rest of the team, however, the story had a happy ending! Suppose this was applied to everything we do. Would the world not be a better place to live in? Just a thought from your friendly, open-minded, wet-nosed, soft-eared neighborhood dog.

A friend of mine told me not so long ago that life was all about give and take. He told me I should be prepared to give him all my bones—everything else he would take. He was joking, of course (I hope), but I have seen that there are humans who appear to believe that they can take and take and take. Barry told me he has even witnessed supervisors at work who seem to feel this is a good way to go: That they can take and take from employees and never give back (either monetary rewards or even verbal recognition). How should we treat these (in my view) misguided soles? A vexing question!

For me, it's all about choices. I am more than willing to help those that have found themselves in situations that limit their ability to choose, and I happily share my treats and bones with them. I have nothing to do, however, with those that choose to take the path of living off others, and demand that giving them material things is their "right." I understand this is easily said and not always so easy to achieve, but I do the best I can. In troublesome cases where a dog will not leave me alone, many times I turn to my friends for advice and support. It is surprising how often this can provide either a different perspective or even a solid solution to my problems. Sometimes help is just a bark away.

To illustrate how many people believe that choices are made from within, I have often heard visitors to our house quote the saying, "God helps those who help themselves." These words are often attributed to The Bible or Benjamin Franklin, but in fact they were written in an article called "Discourses Concerning Government," by Algernon Sidney, an English Whig politician. The article was published in 1698, some 15 years after Sidney, who was considered a martyr for republican government, had been beheaded for treason. In those days, British management certainly were tough on anyone they considered a troublemaker. By way of interest: Franklin "borrowed" the phrase in 1736 when he wrote his *Poor Richard's Almanac*.

The Bible encourages us to help all creatures, regardless of their circumstances or who they are. That said, The Bible also explains that it is okay to ask The Great Dane for help, but that She expects us to take action for ourselves in order to make those wishes come true.

There you have it. Requesting help is sensible but be prepared to put effort into making your dreams and ideas come true. To quote Captain Jean-Luc Picard of the Starship Enterprise: "Make it so!"

INTERLUDE

Bone Break

At this point I would like to introduce Merlin, another member of our family. Merlin is a handsome, gray, Paso Fino horse. The Paso Fino is a naturally gaited horse breed dating back to when horses were imported to the Caribbean from Spain. Paso Finos are prized for their smooth and natural four-beat gait.

Paso Finos are gentle when they are calm—and they are calm when their human companion's attitude is serene. Merlin describes himself as "spirited" when he's feeling particularly lively, at odds with the world, or if Pam or Barry are upset or angry. Horses can be emotional creatures (aren't we all?) and their temperament can be easily affected by the conditions around them, the imbalance of other horses, and, significantly (at least for you guys), the frame of mind of their human companion. I've witnessed on numerous occasions how Merlin will sense either Pam or Barry's state of mind when they arrive at the barn.

Horses will know if you are nervous, frightened, angry, frustrated, or in some other emotional state—and will react accordingly. While this may not be too disastrous most of the time, I have witnessed several occasions when a trainer has told a rider to relax or take a grip on their emotions before getting into the saddle. In extreme cases the trainer has forbidden the rider to mount their steed because the situation could become dangerous for both rider and horse. Personally, if Merlin is in one of his moods I simply stay out of his way. He has that quick, hot, Latin temper—and if he starts snorting and sweating because he's annoyed at something, being the wise boy that I am, I run and hide. I figure you cannot argue with a steam engine.

Merlin got his name because of the kind of magic he uses—or so he says. On a gray, misty morning, or when snow is on the ground, he is almost impossible to see. But when the sun is shining and the grass is green he stands out starkly on the hillsides where he grazes. When he gaits he seems to glide effortlessly over the ground, his long main flowing in the wind. Even I have to admit he does look sort of magical—but don't ever let him know I said this. He already has a large enough ego.

Until recently Pam and Barry were companions to two Paso Finos, but, sadly, Barry's horse, Ramo, died of a very complex and rare type of colic. He was a beautiful smooth-haired brown horse, regal in bearing, larger than most Paso Finos, and a gentle sweetheart. Like Merlin, Ramo's blood could rage when he was irritated or upset, but he rarely showed this side of his character. Barry used to fondly refer to him as the biggest, sweetest dog he has ever known—excluding yours truly, of course.

Even though horses are big, strong animals they are really quite delicate creatures. Horses will often tend to suffer with stomach issues, such as colic, due to their complicated internal plumbing. Legs and feet can also be another area of concern. A horse can easily become lame because of a foot injury, disease, diet, or from a host of other reasons. If they suffer a bad leg fracture there is often nothing that can be done except to put the horse down. I suppose the moral of this story is that just because something seems large, healthy, and strong, there may be unseen weaknesses and sensitivities. That is something to remember, perhaps, when we are dealing with others.

If you have never ridden a Paso you should try one. When gaiting they glide along effortlessly with almost no bouncing for the rider.

Barry often tells of the time he went trail riding with a group of other horses and riders. He was the last but one in the group. When the rider at the front decided to speed things up the group followed suit, including Ramo and Barry. From behind Barry came a howl of laughter. The lady at the rear of the group was laughing so hard she nearly fell off her horse. Later, Barry asked what had amused her so much. "You" she said, explaining that when everyone else had taken off they bounced up and down, but Barry's head had kept dead level. Ramo's feet had simply moved more rapidly in order to keep up with the troop.

The reason for bringing Merlin into the fray is because Barry often uses the social structure and behavior of horses to describe how humans act when at work. Bring a strange horse into the herd and immediately the dynamics of the group change. Those working in any type of organization will recognize immediately how true this is. A new pecking order is established, and, in some cases, the role of an individual horse within the herd may change. Sound familiar at work?

Horses will often have specific jobs to do on behalf of the herd. For example, one will be the sentinel or sentry: the horse who looks for signs of danger. Horses are animals of flight, so once one horse runs the herd generally follows. Of course, there will always be the herd leader—not always the most aggressive or strongest horse but the one that will seek to protect, be the guide, and look after the entire group. It is not uncommon within a herd of wild horses for the leader to be an older mare, since often she is the calmest, wisest, and most experienced horse.

We can learn a lot from horses and their willingness to recognize strengths and weaknesses in each other. Many leadership courses (there are a plethora of them on the internet) utilize horses in self-evaluation assessments, and to teach leadership and team building skills.

Why use horses? A phrase I've heard many times from horse instructors and people in the horse world is, "You can lie to others, you can lie to yourself, but you cannot lie to a horse." Is this true? Ask any human companion to a horse and they would tell you emphatically, "Do not even try to lie to your horse."

As previously mentioned, horses are animals of flight. In their natural habitat they have to depend on their ability to recognize potential danger quickly in order to stay alive. Within the herd they have to learn to trust each other, to communicate clearly, and to know their place in the herd. Leadership and team work is an essential part of a horse's well-being.

A horse will know if you are fearful, lack confidence, or if your leadership skills are weak. Unless a horse relates to you, trusts you, and respects you, he will not follow. You cannot "bluff" a horse—the horse knows all! Horses, like many other animals, rely on instinct, smell, taste, sound, and, above all, body language.

Professor Emeritus of Psychology at UCLA, Albert Mehrabian, has postulated that by far the highest percentage of all human communications are non-verbal. Barry once told me that he cannot lie to Pam because she always knows his intent, even before he does. We think his body language and expression give him away. Either that or Pam is psychic (not that I would put that past her either since, as I can attest, she seems able to read the minds of dogs, too!). Barry never tries to play poker with Pam.

Horses cannot speak, so understanding non-verbal communication is vital to their survival and well-being. Unlike many humans, horses do not role play and will instantly react to your energy and behavior. If you want a horse to co-operate and follow, you must demonstrate leadership. Horses will use their natural abilities to determine if you are to be trusted and have leadership capability. To gain a horse's trust an individual must communicate clearly and effectively (especially non-verbally), face their fears, be willing to "listen" carefully when the horse responds, manage their emotions, and be consistent in their actions. To quote Dwight D. Eisenhower: "Leadership is the art of getting someone else to do something you want done because he wants to do it."

It is for the reasons outlined above that many business schools use horses to teach leadership skills. Horses provide instant, honest feedback. The biggest challenge for many horse companions is to understand their horse through observation. Horses communicate a great deal through their responses and actions, but most humans have problems understanding what they are "saying." From a personal perspective, however, I still believe you cannot go far wrong with a bit of bottom sniffing and tail wagging.

My D.E.V.: Understand that the foundation for both leadership and team building is respect and trust. Managing one's own fears, emotions, and stresses will help you gain personal power and personal respect. Clearly understanding one's own strengths and weaknesses will help the process of personal improvement and understanding of others as you progress along the path toward working with and through others. You can bully people into doing what you want at work, but they will not necessarily respect or trust you. You can demand that people do as you command because of your position of authority or power, but you will not deserve or be given respect or trust. Leadership is about values and demonstration of living to those standards through example. Surround yourself with good folks, and then treat those people with respect and trust—and in return you will receive respect and trust from them. Learn from horses! Look after the interests of the herd, and the herd will look after you. Be honest with yourself and other people. Try talking to a horse!

In talking about using animals as trainers for leadership and lie detectors I can see it's only a matter of time before some bright spark of a chief executive adopts the idea where horses will be brought into job interviews. The horse will be trained to nod or shake its head at the end of the interview signifying "Yay" or "Neigh." Candidates will be handed a poop scooper on their way into the interview. Those who do not clean up at the completion of the process will be automatically disqualified—as will any smart ass who tries to bring in extra hay or treats as bribes.

Exit interviews could also become great fun as horses can help an employee leave a company in style by planting two memento horseshoe marks on the bottom of the departing individual. An additional benefit of using a horse for exit interviews? This could well lead to a reduction in the number of key people willing to hand in their resignation. "You want to voluntarily leave the company? Well then—off to the exit interview you go."

As you can tell, we dogs are always thinking out of the box. Talk to any dog companion to see if their animal has not failed to defeat them on some level or another by doing something completely unexpected. I will quote one very intelligent human, Nora Roberts, who wrote in her book, *The Search*, "Everything I know, I learned from dogs."

MERLIN

THOUGHT FIVE

Gotta Scratch That Itch
~ *Ethics*

Throughout this book I have talked a lot about the importance of trust in establishing long-term and meaningful relationships with other creatures. One way of creating a value system for yourself by which others can determine if you are worthy or not is to always behave in a moral and ethical fashion. Animals instinctively create their own set of ethics according to their circumstances. They don't lie, cheat, or play politics with other creatures. Have you ever known your dog, cat, horse, mouse, or parrot to lie? Animals may use their brainpower to try to get what they want, but animals just don't know how to look you in the eye and deliberately try to deceive you. Has your animal ever stolen from you (not counting food or things to play with, such as socks, which I consider fair game), cheated in some way, or gone behind your back to others?

Humans, on the other hand, seem to need training to develop an ethical behavior that is acceptable in the business world. Larger companies and organizations will most likely have policies, rules, and guidelines to ensure that employees comply with the law of the land and company expectations. I have to tell you guys, as a mere but wonderfully constructed creature, I do not think this speaks highly of your species. I firmly believe that most of us instinctively know right from wrong, although this is usually supplemented by the example set by our parents and other influential souls in our lives. If we do wrong most of us feel guilty, and, like an itch, we want to scratch that guilt so it disappears.

My mother taught me right from wrong as soon as I was born. If I was disrespectful to any of my brothers and sisters I was quickly brought into line when my mum would grab me by the scruff of my neck and place me (gently—because she always reacted with love) to one side. Later, when my teeth came in, if I bit mum too hard—even by accident—she simply stood up and walked away. Lessons are learned quickly when the milk bar leaves of its own accord!

As far as I can see, the ethics training given to a company employee appears to comprise of providing instructions on how they should behave in certain circumstances as a means to ensure the company will not be exposed to breaking the law or be sued for improper practices. Do these instructions give the individual the best ethical guidelines? Not necessarily.

In many cases a company is seeking to avoid trouble for the company rather than growing a culture where ethics and morals are a fundamental part of working for that company. I assume that's why the training is termed "business ethics"—such training only applies to those things that interest the company.

What does the term "ethics" mean to you? For me, ethics are a set of key principles by which my life is guided. This is a much broader definition than that taught in "business ethics" training, where the objective is to follow company guidelines and legal requirements. My principles include honesty, fairness, equality, and respect for diversity and individual rights. I try to apply these principles in all that I do. I try to respect all creatures (even humans, despite all of their problems), to treat them as I would want to be treated, and to be honest with them at all times. In my experience, applying these principles leads to trust from my fellow beings—and trust is a door opener to so many areas in our relationships with others.

Aristotle defined ethics as "practical wisdom." He tried to think about what it takes for a human being to be a "good" person—and no wonder this took some thinking! We animals don't have to wonder about things for so long since we use instinct to help us in such matters. If I have completely understood Aristotle's thoughts, he decided that ethics was a practical rather than a theoretical science. While Aristotle considered that virtue played an important role in the way we develop ethical behavior for ourselves, he concluded that good conduct was born of habit. Habit requires repeated action. Action has to be voluntary—in other words, we have to want to be good. It follows that as we develop our "habits," we also develop self-esteem, and with self-esteem happiness naturally follows.

Could this be the reason I am such a happy dog and wag my tail so much? My experience of watching humans is that wealth, or ownership of worldly things, rarely leads to happiness. I am always willing to share my toys with Katie and Reign, although I have to confess that bones are a "different kettle of fish," as Barry would say. This saying is most apt since I classify bones as "foodstuff"; they do not count as "worldly possessions." Besides, bones don't last long in this world anyway—well, not with me! Still, I must be a *really* good "person." I know this because my companions repeat, over and over, "good boy, Parker, good job"—even if all I'm doing is sitting or going to the bathroom!

Barry, as I already mentioned, is originally from England, so when discussing business ethics he always dusts off his old, tired standby by saying, "Ethics for some companies is next to Suthics." This refers to the fact that the southern United Kingdom counties of Sussex and Essex border each other, and that some Brits talk with a lisp. It's a very British sense of humor thing and it may have been funny once, but after a few times it wears a little thin on the senses. I think he's trying to point out that ethical behavior can be whatever you want it to be, and that some companies may proclaim ethical practices, but in fact only want to avoid trouble or infringement of the law.

Have you ever overheard someone say something detrimental about the working ethical practices of their company? I have. Only the other day I overheard someone explaining that a product shipment did not fully comply with legal requirements. The risk of being caught was low, so instructions were given to ship the equipment since it was the end of a quarter and the sale was needed to fulfill the forecast provided to corporate. Senior management had made it clear to the production team: "Failure to meet the numbers is not an option." That directive sounded to me like the Borg collective in *Star Trek*—scary! So, to avoid problems, managers will often balance the decision between the risks of being found out against the risk of losing their job.

The advice from this boy would be to hold your tail high, dig in your paws—and don't ship just to make sales numbers! If push comes to shove, and someone loses their job because they have honestly tried to comply with the law, the company is unlikely to win an unfair dismissal suit if an employee takes them to court. On the other hand, if the shipment is discovered to be illegal by either the receiving company or an external agency, serious problems may result—for both you and the company!

I would have to question if this is an ethical company with whom I would want to do business. I realize this is an unfair dilemma for many employees, and that companies do not offer rewards to individuals for taking actions that are ethical but not necessarily in the best short-term interests of the company's results. I do believe holding to your own values is important—and that goes back to that old self-esteem thing. Barry told me that during the course of his career there were a couple of times he wished he had spoken up against things with which he fundamentally disagreed—and this still rankles him today. He would like to scratch that itch—but he cannot reach it.

I prefer to use the phrase "moral philosophy" rather than the word "ethics." "Moral philosophy" seems more encompassing and reflects more of what we four-legged folks know to be true—but don't get Barry started about business ethics! He loves to rattle on and on about how managers within companies deliberately withhold information from employees, investors, and others regarding how the company is really performing. Or he might start rambling on about a company representative painting a glowing picture of the company's position while knowing perfectly well clouds are on the horizon that will affect performance. The information is deliberately withheld since it would likely have a damaging effect on the company's image or potentially show weakness—possibly resulting in lowering of the all-important stock price.

Barry really gets quite beside himself when on a roll about managers who deliberately mislead employees, not with outright lying but by not providing relevant information. The intentional result is the employee reaching the wrong conclusion. The act is calculated, is intended to confuse or mislead, and in Barry's book is almost worse than lying because it assumes employees will discover the truth in due course. Managers that deliberately act this way will choose their words very carefully ahead of time so they can show later they did not actually say the words the employees thought they had heard. I am so glad that we animals don't have to face these kinds of problems.

For Barry, misrepresentation, for that is what it is, becomes the ugly side of management. Misrepresentation is immoral and unethical. Unfortunately, misrepresentation appears to also be common in many forms of government. CEOs worldwide are often puzzled at the lack of trust shown by employees, yet we see instance after instance where companies have deliberately cheated or misled their employees, investors, and even government agencies. Laws to prevent this misguidance are becoming tougher, but inevitably lead to higher administration costs for both guilty and innocent companies alike.

I do not believe it is reasonable to expect 100 percent commitment and trust from employees—but then in return decide what information to give them and when, according to how it suits business purposes.

Try going on-line on your computer to review the lists of the most unethical companies in the world. I pawed over a number of lists on the internet from various providers. Did I neglect to tell you how brilliant we Vizslas are? No? I didn't think I had. In the course of my research I was astounded by the number of household names that frequently cropped up in all of the lists. It just made my jaw slobber in amazement and my tail twitch in anger.

As I write this, I am sad to report that three large American corporations are among the Top 10 offenders in almost every single listing reviewed. Another three companies appear frequently in many of the other lists.

I hope this will change over time. The really interesting point is that every major company on the "unethical" list has a stated ethics policy, and all publicly state that ethics training is provided to their employees. Some of the companies have an ethics telephone hotline for both employees and the general public to dial into if they want to complain. Barry reckons the complaints are most likely dropped into "File 13"—his expression for the trash can.

There is some good news though. When I pawed through the list of the most ethical companies, I learned that there are more ethical than unethical companies operating in the world today. I also noted that American companies were in the majority of those that would be added to Santa's "good" list. Perhaps there is hope that, with help from us (we can avoid them at all costs until they make changes), the bad companies will want to be added to the "good" list and will abandon moving to the "dark side." It just takes effort and determination on all our parts.

How can we reach toward high ethical standards of behavior? We dogs know only too well that leadership starts at the top and needs to be demonstrated by example. Canine leaders don't just stand by and let others do their dirty work. Neither does the pack follow a dog they do not trust or respect. The pack would simply vote them out of office—usually by force.

Wouldn't you love to see some CEOs, CFOs, COOs, CTOs, or some other kind of Os ejected from a company with employees biting lumps out of their backsides, legs, neck, hands, and other body parts as they run out the door? Oooh, what a delicious thought!

Is all modern business run by immoral management? No! Barry often talks about the years he worked for Juergen, a gentleman who owned his own company and whose word was his bond. Every employee in that company, every vendor, and every customer knew that once Juergen had given a verbal promise he would follow through. Even though, in hindsight, Juergen may have made an error that would be detrimental to himself, he would honor his promise no matter the cost to him or the company. A written agreement, or even a handshake, was not necessary.

Barry believes that many written agreements are rarely worth much anyway since corporation lawyers often work hard to ensure there are as many exclusion clauses as possible. Sometimes the wording is deliberately misleading to ensure open interpretation—and unenforceable except in the favor of the corporation issuing the agreement. Strangely enough: The legal departments in large companies are intimately involved with preparing the ethics policies. Perhaps folks in legal should be the first ones to be sent for ethics training?

Was Juergen ever taken advantage of? Absolutely! Those people or companies with low ethical boundaries would not hesitate to take this man's generous nature and turn things to their own advantage.

Barry, who witnessed this on several very notable occasions, once asked Juergen how he felt about this. Juergen replied that he was more than aware that about 10 percent of those he dealt with would take advantage. He forgave them, for they did more damage to themselves, both in their own eyes and in the eyes of others, than to him. In fact, Juergen's reputation for keeping his word, no matter the consequences, was enforced.

Some folks worried about Juergen's perceived naivety. The point for Juergen, however, was that 90 percent of people or companies would not take advantage or try to cheat him. This meant Juergen could hold his head up proudly and be confident that his own actions were honest and ethical. That said, once Juergen had been cheated the trust bond was broken, and as Chuck Berry once said, "Don't let the same dog bite you twice." As a canine, I couldn't agree more. Once bitten twice shy!

Barry's opinion is that Juergen's honesty in his dealings with others resulted in a form of modern "pay it forward." Barry said he never failed to feel humble when those that had been on the receiving end of Juergen's philosophy and integrity returned that favor many times over. Employees trusted Juergen and openly supported the company when times were hard. Vendors did their best to satisfy his every need. Customers remained loyal to the company and friends were friends for life.

I hope you feel the same conviction in your managers' or company's honesty and integrity—because honesty and integrity instill solid levels of confidence. Oh, by the way, when you look up that list of the most ethical companies trading today, try looking back in their history. I'm willing to bet that you will find the driving force behind the vast majority of these companies was not to make profit or to raise shareholder value. And yet, because the companies had passion, belief, and integrity, shareholder value *did* rise.

Another reason for the success of many of the companies I have reviewed was a desire, in some way, to make the world a better place. The companies needed to be profitable—after all, without profit the companies would cease to exist—but the profits and consequent advantages to shareholders came from that initial driving force to do something positive for the world. In so doing those companies brought benefit to many.

Not only for-profit companies ignore ethical and moral behavior. These days you cannot help but read about not-for-profit or charitable organizations that are using donations to support a well-paid internal bureaucracy. In many cases, little money, if any, passes to the declared beneficiary. Pam reckons these are the most dishonorable people alive since they intend to seduce ordinary people into thinking they are contributing money for the good of their fellow men, children, or animal friends. Playing on the emotions of others this way has to be the lowest form of behavior possible. The good news is that you can check the less-desirable charities on the internet before paying over any money. If funding organizations call Pam she always asks them to confirm in writing how much of her contribution will be paid to the charity. The number of telephone calls we receive is dwindling!

The D.E.V.: In this humble dog's opinion, trust is the most vital ingredient of leadership. How can a leader lead if the troops will not trust to follow in that person's footsteps? Once broken, trust is difficult to win back. The old saying that trust is earned, not given, is so true—and holds true with pets, too! To quote the award-winning French author, filmmaker, magician, and poet Michel Houellebecq: "The love of a dog is a pure thing. He gives you a trust which is total. You must not betray it." So don't!

The giving and receiving of trust can be extremely positive and rewarding. You will not be disappointed with results if you treat your fellow employees, customers, and vendors with respect and honesty while honoring promises made to them. That is the way we animals treat each other. There will always be those who will not respond well. Try to avoid such people, and, if possible, strike them out of your life. Resist the temptation to fall to their level. The success these folks may enjoy from time to time through cheating or lying will come back to haunt them one day.

One last thought before we leave the subject of ethics and morals, and one that must receive very serious consideration. The wise and respected leader, Mahatma Gandhi, once said, "The greatness of a nation and its moral progress can be judged by the way its animals are treated." America: You know what to do! I'm ready to accept whatever bones you want to toss in my direction with humility and love.

THOUGHT SIX

Hmmm—Who's in Charge
~ *Leadership versus Management*

I **was talking to Merlin the other day** and he was explaining that, for horses, leadership is all about vision. In horse terms, this means the leader will keep the herd safe, watered, and well fed by understanding what is necessary to achieve the objective. Horses instinctively turn toward the leader, or Alpha horse, and in many herds this is often an older mare.

In the wild, the stallion manages the herd, keeping intruders away from his mares, running behind the herd to make sure there is no immediate danger and to ensure slower horses keep up with the rest of the herd. In domesticated herds, where humans have castrated the males, geldings are usually accepted by the herd as both leaders and managers if an appropriate female is not part of the herd. Barry believes the practice of castration could prove very handy in some company organizations—with the added benefit of almost completely eliminating the need for training in sexual harassment.

Horses clearly understand that the biggest, strongest, most aggressive horse may not necessarily be the best leader for the herd. Rather, horses prefer a calm, experienced equine that has the best understanding of the needs for the entire herd.

Merlin is part of a mixed herd of both mares and geldings. The son of one of the mares, a gelding named Rowdy (a most apt handle for this boy), is both assertive and aggressive. In fact, Rowdy is certainly number two in the pecking order—but it is his mother, Alexis, with her much sweeter nature, who is the leader of the herd.

Human partners to the rest of the herd give Rowdy a very wide berth since he has been known to be aggressive to them, too. If Rowdy forgets his position in the herd, however, his mother soon puts him in his place. Pam told me this is often true in the human world, where mothers have to correct their children when they get out of hand. My mother was a loving, gentle soul, but I rediscovered all too quickly why they call female dogs "bitches" if I ever did something to which she objected.

This magnificent and self-effacing specimen of a canine believes that the relationship between the gelding, Rowdy, and his mother, Alexis, is a simple example of the difference between a leader and a manager. Managers certainly need leadership skills in order to coax the best performance possible from others in the herd, but there can only be one true herd leader. The leader needs to have a vision and be able to clearly communicate that vision in an inspirational way so that others can follow with conviction. The best leaders lead by example, are prepared to delegate responsibility to others, and use coaching and mentoring to achieve the maximum performance from those around them.

I have never heard Alexis talking to the other horses, so I can only imagine how she would convey her vision to the herd, but I suspect she might say: "I see luscious green grass for us to eat, an open field with clean water running through it, and an environment where we can be safe from all dangers. Follow me and I will lead you to this wonderful land."

Unfortunately, even if Alexis does manage to lead the others to this horse heaven, humans will always want to interfere. I have often heard, when I have been at the horse barn with Pam and Barry, a human partner of a horse say something like: "My horse is getting too fat. I need to put a grazing muzzle on." A grazing muzzle is an instrument of horse torture that is wrapped around the face and mouth of the horse. It usually has a small hole at the mouth end of this devilish contraption to allow the horse to eat, while restricting the intake of grass. Merlin, and some of the others in his herd, are smart though, and use trees, fences, or even their legs and hooves to remove the mask—much to the chagrin (and to the cost) of their human companions.

To be fair to humans, though, they are trying to look after the best interests of their equine friends. Humans cite the reason for the use of a grazing muzzle is to prevent their companion horse from becoming too fat on the rich (sugary) green grass. A fat horse can contract laminitis (inflammation of sensitive layers of tissue inside the hoof of the horse). Laminitis can result in a very lame horse. I think this is an excuse for humans so that they don't have to adjust the girth of their saddle if the horse "expands" a little. Lazy creatures, humans, unlike dogs who must work much harder. How do I know this? Every time, when Pam returns home from a difficult and tiring day at work, she will say, "I had to work like a dog today." Need I say more?

Do humans get fat like horses when they get too much of the good stuff? I've heard Barry refer to managers who have had an easy run to the top of their profession and who exploit their position accordingly for their own benefit (even to the detriment of the company and other employees) as "fat cats." I like "fat cats"—because they cannot run as fast. Thinner cats tire me out!

According to Barry, some businesses, just like the herd, also suffer the "human interaction" effect. This includes demands from investors, shareholders, banks, senior corporate managers, or other interested parties who would appreciate more of the "crispy ones" to pass their way by reducing costs within the business. In order to increase or protect profits, management is often forced to introduce the "grazing muzzle." Unfortunately, the financial "grazing muzzle" often adversely affects a number of employees who may lose their jobs as expenses are reduced. I'm not sure there is much anyone can do to prevent these things from happening, except to encourage leaders to seek a friendly "tree" or "fence." You can always use your "hooves" and "legs" to get rid of the muzzle, but not everyone can afford to leave their jobs every time one of these demands to reduce cost is reflected through the company.

Many jobs require leadership skills. The best path toward encouraging staff to acquire and improve leadership skills is to use performance reviews, personal development training, mentoring, coaching, or other practices. Group leaders, managers, and supervisors need to draw on their leadership skills if they are to maximize the potential performance of the employees that report to them.

Employees who know they are doing their job well gain satisfaction and confidence from the knowledge they are giving of their best. When employees enjoy their jobs, the managers who helped them to improve also gain a deep sense of satisfaction and fulfillment. Remember: Don't be shy about asking for help or advice from your boss if you feel that your leadership skills need improvement. After all, the whole purpose of my wonderfully wise and insightful teachings is to make sure you love your job and have more fun at work.

There is a tendency in certain groups to only value those employees who demonstrate a strong desire to become leaders, or who want to acquire leadership skills. In my very humble but oh-so-right opinion, some of the larger companies tend to overly emphasize the need for *all* their employees to become "leaders."

There can be only one leader of the herd. It is true many herd members will need leadership skills in order to effectively fulfill their mission within the herd, but not everyone wants, or even needs, to develop leadership skills to manage others. Everyone needs skills to manage and lead themselves—but that might be as far as it goes. That does not mean the folks who do not want to be leaders are of lesser value to the company. On the contrary, Barry told me he knows of many valuable employees who love what they do, are good at their job, are very hard workers, but have no ambition beyond the horizon of doing their job well.

If led correctly, every employee should have a solid feeling of belonging and of value. Looking for successors to lead the company and seeking to encourage the benefits of the use of leadership skills throughout the company are natural, worthy, and noble causes to pursue. It should be recognized, though, that not everyone has leadership capability, and many do not wish to become a leader..

An example that comes to mind of how some souls do not necessarily enjoy leadership roles is the story that was told to me not so long ago by a horse called Georgina. The lovely Georgina told me that for a short while, after the death of the leading mare, and because no one else would take on the job, she became the leader of their small herd.

She hated her new leadership role but recognized someone had to step up to the plate or there would be chaos. She was miserable—for the mantle of leadership did not fit well with her. She was lucky, however, because her human companion recognized her sadness—particularly when they rode together. Georgina was far less responsive than in the past.

Georgina's human, however, *misread* the signals, thinking that Georgina was lonely. Georgina's human decided to bring in a buddy for her, and so Grace was introduced into the field. Georgina disliked Grace from the start. Grace immediately began taking over as herd leader. Georgina was more than happy to pass on the reins (no pun intended) to Grace and within a remarkably short time the herd accepted and settled down to its new leadership. Georgina was extremely grateful to Grace, even though she did not like her and would not buddy up to her. Soon Georgina was back to her normal fun-loving self.

Eventually, Georgina's human companion observed the adjustment in Georgina's demeanor following the change of leadership and finally cottoned on to what had happened. The key in this story is that the herd needed a leader, and Georgina stepped into the role through necessity, but not because she felt comfortable with the role, and certainly not because she wanted to be the herd leader.

Georgina's situation was resolved for her through lucky circumstances. Be careful not to accept a leadership role or position if you neither want it nor feel comfortable doing it just because the company "expects" it of you. Your supervisor will respect your decision provided he or she is worth his or her salt. (Did you know that in olden times salt was used to reward workers? Hence the word "salary," which comes from the Latin *salarium*—the amount a soldier was paid to buy salt). Be prepared to fully embrace the responsibility if you take the new leadership position. Be forewarned, however, if you take the job for purely monetary or status reasons: Experience shows that accepting increased levels of responsibility without full and complete commitment usually ends in failure. You could find yourself without a job at all if you cannot give of your best in an enthusiastic manner.

Good managers understand how to motivate employees. Strong managers and leaders listen to their staff, actively welcome open dialogue, and provide tools so everyone can perform to maximum efficiency. Excellent managers and leaders absorb and act upon valuable inputs, accept constructive criticism as a positive opportunity for improvement, have faith that people will always try to do their best, and value and inspire those that work for them.

Many employees feel they are victim to the whims of their supervisor or company management. The truth is that everyone can participate in management and leadership processes by approaching their jobs positively and offering proactive feedback to their superiors. I'm not asking everyone to be a "teacher's pet" (although you should seriously consider this as I love being the pet to my teachers, especially when juicy bones may be at "steak"), nor am I suggesting that you start criticizing everything in the company.

Try to suggest a sensible solution when you are offering feedback. If you can recognize a problem, you are probably the best one to suggest a way toward resolution—but remember to be realistic. Don't tell a manager that the staff is unhappy and the best solution is to give everyone a 50 percent raise—that's unreasonable. Outrageous suggestions devalue your sincerity. Seek solutions that can be acceptable to all parties. I'm not suggesting you should back down from presenting painful solutions—but be sure to present wisely.

Avoid aggressive feedback presentations as this will only engender defensiveness. Simply state the facts in a pleasant way—and don't expect an instant response. Pam's boss, for example, does not always react straightaway to any feedback. Instead, he likes to take several days, and sometimes weeks, to think things through, take advice if necessary, and then make the changes he deems appropriate.

Some leaders have wonderful vision, can communicate this vision in a clear and unambiguous way, can inspire and motivate—and yet are not the best managers. For example, entrepreneurs in small companies often lead and grow their company to success. Problems can start, however, when the company grows to the point where it becomes impossible for one person to handle all of the decision-making processes without detrimentally affecting company performance.

Some entrepreneurs have difficulty in delegating responsibility because they believe they alone have generated the company's success. In the beginning, the decision-making tree was short, and decisions were made quickly and efficiently. Wise leaders, however, know instinctively when to begin to delegate responsibility to others who can be trusted to implement necessary processes and carry out certain tasks that will improve company performance.

The best leaders and managers appreciate and reward a job well done. Remember that praise or recognition of good performance is one of the strongest rewards an employee can receive. Do not underestimate those that make their job look easy or work quietly to achieve results. These folks are often the among company's most valuable employees.

The best leaders and managers lead by example. Make sure the examples are good ones, though, since many employees will also follow examples of bad behavior, too. Use messages to communicate both internally and externally but be careful not to fall into the trap of believing your own press.

Many companies use vision or mission statements to communicate their purpose, but over time this message is lost—or even turns into a negative if the statement is without any real meaning or is just a "wish list." Many mission statements don't achieve their intent. For example, here is a mission statement issued by a company owning a chain of grocery stores: "To create a shopping experience that pleases our customers, a workplace that creates opportunities and a great working environment for our associates, and a business that achieves financial success." On the surface the statement embodies everything a person could ask for, but Barry snorted at this statement and reckoned he could summarize this as: "Create Utopia and make a lot of money in the process." Barry went on to further illustrate his thinking by saying it was rather like the response from a beauty pageant queen when asked the question, "What matters most to you?" Her answer? "World peace." Nice thought, but no substance. You know, Barry might have a point. My question would be: "What differentiates this company from others?"

Encouraging leadership values requires mentoring—because mentors help individuals recognize and develop their natural skills and then reach their full potential. Improving management capability, however, seems to me to be also a matter of providing as many tools for the tool box as possible.

Great leaders and managers automatically adopt a process of continuous improvement as part of their learning program. Pam is a part-time dental hygienist. She is a very good dental hygienist. She also runs an animal therapy business, and works on a wide variety of creatures, including canines, equines, birds, goats, pigs—and even Barry! She is a natural leader and healer. When Pam first started her business, in her mid-50s no less, she lacked confidence because she just did not have many of the processes and skills to be totally proficient in the work she loves so much. Clearly, it is this love of being able to help the animals that makes her so good at what she does. Animals instinctively know about a person. Have I mentioned before that animals are smarter than humans? I believe I may have!

Pam could not be successful in her activities without full commitment and her ability to absorb knowledge. Pam has always been fully committed to being the best dental hygienist she could be—and she received a great deal of training before being allowed to start practicing her craft. But Pam had no training for her animal business—so she started to read everything available on the subject. She attended a variety of different training courses, carefully selected and researched for their quality of approach to the subject at hand and their reputation among her professional community. The more Pam learned, the more her confidence grew.

When Pam returned home from her training courses, I would lay on her lap while she stroked my head and ears in that comforting way she has. What struck me as she confided her thoughts to me was that she had gained a much better understanding as to the secret of the success of those that taught the classes. The teachers appeared confident, yet all of the teachers admitted that they learned new things every single day—and that they incorporated these new lessons into their work. New learning kept the teachers fresh, excited, and allowed them to continue to enjoy their work. The teachers had adopted a process of continuous improvement. These teachers learned from students, colleagues, peers—but the best mentors were the animals!

Change is vital to the continued health of companies—and the best leaders and managers should always be open to change—but everyone must resist making change just for the sake of change. As my wise and funny colleague, Snoopy, once said, "Sometimes when I get up in the morning, I feel very peculiar. I feel like I've just got to bite a cat! I feel like if I don't bite a cat before sundown, I'll go crazy! But then I just take a deep breath and forget about it. That's what is known as real maturity."

Leaders make mistakes like everyone else—but great leaders turn their failures into positives by learning to learn from their mistakes. Leaders encourage others to do the same. Many of our most decorated leaders, including Steve Jobs, Bill Gates, Henry Ford, Walt Disney, Donald Trump, Soichiro Honda, Henry John Heinz, and so many more have experienced catastrophic failures in the early part of their careers—but used the lessons learned moving forward to their successful advantage.

I would like to offer a further thought relating to failure that comes from our very dear departed friend, Bobby Drinnon. People often referred to Bobby as a psychic, but he told Pam and Barry he preferred to be called "an intuitive counselor." Bobby was an extraordinary man who brought comfort and direction to so many people. Bobby died not too long ago after he lost his fight against cancer. Our friend, teacher, and mentor is sorely missed. He once told Pam and Barry to regard perceived failure or rejection as a positive, not a negative. His thinking was that when these things happen they are for a purpose. He always said: "Protection—not rejection."

We should all be able to relate to the mantra of "protection—not rejection" at points in our lives. In our family, what initially appeared to be a negative event, such as a lost job, lost friend, or lost bone, often turns out to be a blessing in disguise. I know how difficult it can be when "disaster" strikes—but time passing often reveals the positive reasons behind such events.

The following Chinese proverb makes the point very well:

> "This Chinese story is about a farmer who used an old horse to till his fields. One day, the horse escaped into the hills and when the farmer's neighbors sympathized with the old man over his bad luck, the farmer replied, 'Bad luck? Good luck? Who knows?' A week later, the horse returned with a herd of horses from the hills and this time the neighbors congratulated the farmer on his good luck. His reply was, 'Good luck? Bad luck? Who knows?'
>
> Then, when the farmer's son was attempting to tame one of the wild horses, he fell off its back and broke his leg. Everyone thought this very bad luck. Not the farmer, whose only reaction was, 'Bad luck? Good luck? Who knows?' Some weeks later,

the army marched into the village and conscripted every able-bodied youth they found there. When they saw the farmer's son with his broken leg, they let him off. Now was that good luck or bad luck? Who knows?

Everything that seems on the surface to be an evil may be a good in disguise. And everything that seems good on the surface may really be an evil. So we are wise when we leave it to God to decide what is good fortune and what misfortune, and thank him that all things turn out for good with those who love him."

The attributes described above are great but the question remains: What makes a leader a great leader? Being the cunning and smart canine that I am I thought I would garner opinion from other folks. To my astonishment, I found a huge variance in thinking among the populace about the type of attributes leaders must possess if they are to be successful. Reign thinks that decisiveness is the most important quality for a leader to exhibit (she likes instruction), Katie believes leaders should have *good communication skills* (she loves to communicate her loving nature through cuddling), while Merlin states categorically that *strategic planning* (such as finding the right type of grass for him to eat) is by far the most critical attribute for a leader. (I'm not particularly surprised by Merlin's response since he is always hungry.)

In light of the differing opinions, I thought I would put together the Top 10 attributes possessed by most of the superb leaders that I know. Some of the headings are very different from any of the ideas that were given to me and at first you may be a little shocked at my choices—but I will try to explain a little, in terms humans can relate to, about why I use these words. So here goes: Parker's List of the 10 Most Valuable Attributes of a Pack Leader:

1. They Have A Nose for What Can Be

The leader of the pack needs to be creative and original. In human terms: The leader is a visionary who passionately believes in what the company is doing and where the company is going. Without vision, direction, and passion the pack will soon find itself lost and surrounded by predators. Leaders of successful commercial companies do not state their vision as: "To get very, very rich with the least amount of effort." Barry told me those that do state such missions are known as "criminals" and usually end up in something called "prison." The best leaders are driven by a passion to do what they enjoy, to fill a need, to have fun—and to make the world a better place.

2. They Have a Bark Worth Listening to
Leaders must communicate effectively. Leaders must share their message so that pack members understand and feel part of the group as it develops, grows, and moves forward. Leaders use "positivity" (a new word I discovered on the internet) to convey their message. In other words, a bark is worth a thousand whines. Barry always says, "Leaders must be inspirational, not perspirational. They should be prepared to walk the talk." Poor lad, he thinks making up words that sound similar matters! Leaders must lead by example. A loud bark without meaning is just that—loud and annoying. Leaders should avoid being labeled "barking mad" by others in the pack.

3. They Have an Arrogant Swagger of the Tail
Leaders must demonstrate confidence, and, yes, perhaps a modest amount of arrogance. Winners have to believe they can win. That does not mean arrogance should overwhelm the leader's ability to listen and learn from others, or that the leader is not prepared to change direction when danger threatens. Having faith is important to achieve results. Leaders need to have a strong yet humble ego. Leaders may not have the ability to listen or accept ideas from others without a healthy dose of humility.

4. They Have a Trustworthy Howl
Leaders must have integrity and honesty—or else they cannot develop trust inside or outside of the pack. Trust is such a meaningful and powerful word. Many things can be achieved with mutual trust: The herd or pack will follow and results will follow, too. Leaders must earn trust over time and demonstrate they are worthy of trust through their approach and actions. Honesty and integrity are the foundations for

building trust—but total trust derives from many aspects of how the leader thinks and acts.

5. They Adopt a Nose Forward, Paw Up, Ears Up, Pointed Tail, Alert Position
Leaders must be focused and results oriented. A leader must have patience and understand that building a great team takes time and effort—but a leader should not have infinite patience. Leaders cannot wait forever or his or her business will not survive. The best leaders encourage others to remain focused so that objectives can be met in a timely fashion and to ensure the group stays "on point" and are not misled by meandering off the chosen path (as I often do!). Vizslas are pointers. When we Vizslas see an animal in the undergrowth we instantly "adopt the position," stand perfectly still, and wait for our human companion to reach us to let us know what they would like us to do next. Teamwork!

6. They Have the Ability to Throw Bones to Others
Leaders must surround themselves with good and trustworthy folks—and leaders should be prepared to delegate responsibility. Pack members develop ownership when given responsibility—and pack members gain confidence and enjoy their jobs more when they "own the work." Treat others as you would wish to be treated yourself. Wise people often refer to the ripple effect of when a stone is thrown into a pond. The ripple may take some time to reach the outer areas of the pond, and the ripple may diminish with distance, but the effect is still there.

7. They Listen to the Rumbling of Their Own Stomach
Leaders must trust their intuition and their "gut." Leaders cannot always use logic or presented facts as the only way to choose a path. Most leaders will know if something feels right or not. Leaders may not always understand why they feel this way when something is not as it should be, but leaders learn to trust their instincts. Leaders learn to overcome the fear of failure because they believe in what they are doing. If they do experience failure, they learn from that experience and turn it to their advantage.

8. They Have a Clear Understanding of Where the Food Comes From
Dogs, and most other animals, are very aware of who, or what, feeds them. We three Vizslateers jump up and down and run around in circles with excitement at feeding time. We leave Pam and Barry in no doubt as to how much we appreciate them giving us our daily "bread." Leaders have a natural understanding about who feeds them. For humans who want to earn their bread, only the investor, the government agency, the boss, the end user, the purchaser, or whoever the internal or external "customer" might be can provide nourishment. Leaders create a vision of what will allow their customers to experience pleasure, and, by working through others, make that pleasurable experience happen. I understand that as the company grows, some employees will lose contact with the all-important external customer— so look for a new customer! Most likely the new "customer" will be inside the company. This could be another department that relies upon your output, your supervisor who needs your support, or some other person or group who depend upon your expertise. It is my strong belief that only customer-oriented groups (no matter who the "customer" might be) are the ones who will succeed and enjoy longevity.

9. They Have a Twinkle in Their Eyes
The strongest leaders have a sense of humor. Humor can be used to achieve so much! Humor creates camaraderie among pack members and helps diffuse sensitive situations—and often can be used to make a point without causing offense. Best of all? Humor can be part of the pack culture to make work more enjoyable. Laughter triggers the release of endorphins, the body's natural chemical that makes us feel good. Laughter decreases stress, increases immune cells, and builds antibodies to help the immune system. Laughter can even temporarily relieve pain, such as that experienced during a performance review—or when my bone is taken away.

10. They Are Able to Resist Biting—Yet Use Their Growl to Good Effect
Leaders must pay heed to the saying that "patience is a virtue." We live in a society of instant gratification, but the reality for the leader is that things take time if a lasting organization is to be built. The dilemma

for the leader is that goals and objectives must be set with reasonable timelines and deadlines in order to achieve sustainable business results. I suppose you could say leaders need to be "patiently impatient."

Pam and Barry swear, despite all the things they do wrong, that they have a guardian angel that looks after them, and that The Big Guy (by which I assume they mean The Great Dane) always has purpose to everything. My dogged objective is to try to the leave this earth the better for having me as part of its life. Should that not be the objective for us all?

The D.E.V.: Leadership and management can often be different "animals," and it is important to understand and respect the difference if we are to maximize our effect on the world. Not every leader is necessarily the best manager, and not every manager is necessarily the best leader. The herd or pack needs a leader—but also good managers as well in order to be successful. Leaders create and motivate. Managers can be creative and should motivate, too, but typically managers must be more consistent, disciplined, and process oriented. Most managers need to use and develop leadership skills to assemble and lead a team of competent and well-motivated employees—but some of the best middle managers are not always visionaries.

Leaders have a positive vision of what they want to achieve—and they communicate this vision effectively both inside and outside of the company or group. Leaders are able to "sell" their vision to inspire and motivate others to follow. Leaders may not always be the best managers but, as the pack grows, smart leaders relinquish responsibilities to trusted people who can perform certain duties better than they can.

Love what you do and treat failure as an opportunity to learn and improve. Believe in yourself and learn from everything around you—since all that you see and hear is a lesson.

Above all: Be virtuous. The famous Chinese philosopher Confucius said: "Virtue is more to man than either water or fire. I have seen men die from treading on water and fire, but I have never seen a man die from treading the course of virtue." Parker says: "Every dog will have his day." No! Don't laugh! Plato himself said, "A dog has the soul of a philosopher."

Leadership has many meanings—including learning how to lead yourself. Leaders must show constraint but also must be prepared to take action when things do not move along as planned. Leaders should understand when to be forgiving and when not to be. Tolerance can be shown in certain circumstances but behaviors that could affect team performance should never be tolerated. Leaders should avoid making change just for the sake of change.

Everyone can contribute to company performance by approaching their jobs in a positive way and by supporting the pack. I can say for certain that puppies are irresistible when they are enthusiastic—and they always provide a lot of feedback on how much they are enjoying playing with me. Try being a puppy: You, too, could be irresistible and loveable—and you just might enjoy your job more, too!

Thought Seven

Herd Selection
~ *Employment*

A **nimals rarely experience the luxury of selecting who is part of their herd.** They have to live with, and make do with, those who are members of the herd—but there will be times when the herd will shun or expel a wrongdoer from their midst, and, of course, injured or sick animals unfortunately may fall foul to predators. The good news is that these events generally are to the benefit of the health of the herd as a unit.

Barry was once told by his friend Juergen, "Use the staff that you have first before you make change for change's sake, but don't be afraid to quickly and decisively change out those people who could be detrimental to the performance of the group." I agree with Juergen. I'm a pretty easygoing guy, so I rarely have problems in playing and staying friends with the dogs I regularly meet—but if I don't like a particular dog because they don't smell right or feel good to me, then I don't allow them to be close to me.

Some corporations have a policy of continual employee turnover in order to keep skill bases current and ideas fresh in the company. There is nothing wrong in this approach—although I find it surprising that some of these same companies expect their employees to be totally loyal, even when jobs are in jeopardy.

In business, it is my understanding that herd selection is made after applicants for a position undergo something called an "interview." Of course, a candidate might happen to be a close relative of one of the senior members of the company, in which case something Barry refers to as "nepotism" creeps in. Nepotism sounds like a pretty ugly disease to me. The purpose of the interview appears to be to select or reject candidates on the basis of their suitability for a particular position. Most candidates feel they have to impress the interviewer, even if they know the position is not ideal for them. Some interviewers feel they need to sell the vacancy and the company to the candidate. In his book, "How to Win Friends and Influence People," Dale Carnegie wrote, "One reason why birds and horses are happy is because they are not trying to impress other birds and horses."

In my view, if both parties agree at the beginning of the interview that the objective is to see if the candidate has the appropriate skills, education, and attitude for the position—and the job, remuneration, and company are right for candidate—the chances of a happy, long-term relationship are enhanced by an order of magnitude.

Barry confided in me that he tried to avoid using the word "interview" if he could. If he was in contact with a potential team member, he preferred to suggest both parties get together for a "chat" or "discussion" in order to "review" the position available in the company. This sounded to me like a typical "Brit" thing, but he claims he did this for two reasons. First, when asked to attend an interview, most candidates have a preconceived idea about what this entails. The interview is just too formal and both sides work too hard in an effort to "sell" themselves or their company to the other party. A "chat" or "discussion" is less formal. Most applicants are more relaxed and inclined to reveal more of themselves if the meeting is less structured. Second, the word "interview" establishes the "box" based on the job description. The word "review" seemed to Barry to imply that there was flexibility in how the position would be administered and filled.

I would suggest that you look for the strengths within a candidate rather than for weaknesses. Barry told me that many "interviewers" considered that strengths would be obvious and apparent, but that part of their task was to discover weaknesses. Barry found during his "chats" with candidates that they often possessed skills and abilities not identified in their resumes or CVs (Curriculum Vitaes) that could prove useful in the course of their job. The reason for this is that many candidates have preconceived ideas of what the company is looking for in the position on offer—and candidates often tailor their inputs accordingly.

I would urge you not to pass up those who you think are truly excellent but may offer a challenge as far as being managed is concerned. Juergen invariably brought people into his organization who were brilliant in their chosen field but could be difficult to manage. Most of these souls were rejected by other companies as potential disruptions to operations. Of course, trying to manage difficult people doesn't always work. One must be prepared and act accordingly. Juergen put together a brilliant team of well-motivated engineers that were the cream of the industry. To be fair, Juergen had a gift of understanding the sensitivities of these folks and what made them tick. For most humans, managing these people can prove frustrating and time consuming. However, once you learn how to navigate these particular seas, the path forward can be both rewarding and beneficial for all concerned.

As the famous horse dressage trainer and rider Lendon Gray once said, "It is the difficult horses that have the most to give to you." This lady has an outstanding record of taking difficult, seemingly unremarkable horses and turning them into superb performance athletes.

Barry once remarked to Juergen, "We have one guy who is hell-bent on falling into the deepest hole possible. How the heck can we manage him?" Juergen's response was simple. "Your job as a manager is not to stop him falling into holes. You cannot stop people wanting to experience what happens when you fall in a hole. The more you put fences around the holes the more these types of characters will want to fall in one. Your job as a manager is to select the holes they fall into. Fence off the deepest ones where they have no chance of getting out, but don't stop them falling into a hole they can climb out of. Once they have experienced the pain of falling in, and the effort it requires to climb out, they will want to avoid falling into holes in the future." Sage advice indeed.

I have successfully used this philosophy on puppies who seem determined to end their young lives as soon as possible. The old saying states that curiosity killed the cat, but I have to wonder if whoever dreamed up this statement ever had a new puppy. Human kids can be a handful—but puppies are in a league of their own! I sometimes let the most curious puppies eat something that tastes awful but I know will do them no harm—or I let them get into a minor skirmish with a cat! It's amazing how quickly puppies settle down to just playing with their toys after understanding that cats come armed with inbuilt weapons.

Suitability to the position intrigues me most. There are pay scales and seniority levels in most corporations determined by the type of job an individual performs and the responsibilities attached to that job. This results in a job description: a standard to which a candidate is matched. I am very familiar with this concept.

Humans parade us at what they call "dog shows," although I refer to them as Human Ego Festivals (or HEFS for short). We dogs are groomed, paraded around a ring, and then made to stand in awkward positions while another human decides if we match a standard for our particular breed. The standard is a written description that states what the ideal should be for a specific breed, bearing in mind the purpose for which the dog has been bred. This particular torture is called "Conformation."

I have met dogs that actually like performing Conformation and going to HEFS. Personally, I think these dogs need psychological help, but as I always say, each to his own. I know Barry feels the same way because he says attending dog shows for him is like watching paint dry. That is unless one of us wins. Then he is enthusiastic! Humans can be so contrary at times!

Being judged against a standard matches precisely what a job interview is all about in many companies. Someone thinks up a title, then writes down the standard for a specific function against which all candidates are judged. The candidate that most closely resembles the standard wins, providing of course the interviewer gets along with the candidate. Usually this means the one that most resembles the interviewer.

Consistency is important, but too much consistency can eliminate some excellent job applicants. Candidates may have strengths and skills well-suited to the majority of tasks to be performed but perhaps lack experience or knowledge in one specific area. Shouldn't a manager developing a team be prepared to trade the strengths of one member of the team against the weaknesses of another? This method may be a little risky—but building a team means being flexible in your thinking! I think the results far outweigh the risks. Barry reckons that strict adherence to standards results in managers ignoring highly talented individuals who cannot exactly fit the profile.

Barry told me that he often calls ORG (Organization) charts "AAAGH" charts. Barry explained that ORG charts are useful for showing hierarchy and responsibilities, especially as the company grows, but he firmly believes ORG charts should never drive how a company works. Barry believes there is always room to be flexible.

Team building is an art as well as a science. ORG chart flexibility should be viewed as a strength and not a weakness. One of the best groups Barry ever worked for did not even have an ORG chart. Everyone understood they had special talents to complete defined tasks and worked with their colleagues to ensure the jobs got done. My feeling is that this can work well in a small group or company, but there needs to be more structure as company grows.

Barry once tried to draw an ORG chart for Merlin's herd of horses. Inevitably, the lead mare, as head of the herd, was CEO (Chief Equine Officer). Her son, the herd manager, was the CFO (Chief Field Officer), an older gelding was the CSO (Chief Social Officer)—and Merlin was HSO (Head Security Officer). Everyone else simply was!

So how do job descriptions come to pass? I suppose the ideal is to write down all of the tasks that need to be accomplished, prioritize these tasks, consider what skills and education are needed to complete the tasks, and then write a job description around these factors. For completeness you can add a title, which really is an indicator to the outside world (and internally for larger groups) of what this job is likely to entail and the seniority within the organization. Unfortunately, what often happens is that the title comes first (from the dreaded AAAGH chart)—and then a vanilla job description is used from past records.

Barry said he's actually seen a job description for a position sent to a manager by Human Resources where HR did not even talk to the manager about the needs for his department! Someone had resigned, the position carried a job title, and this in turn carried with it a generic job description. The job description supplied was the standard by which the manager would be expected to choose his new employee—but things had changed in the manager's department since the job and title had originally been assigned some years before. The department manager saw an opportunity to implement new and different functionality into the tasks for the job. HR, however, was having none of it! The AAAGH chart clearly showed the title in the box—and that title carried a job description. Since the posting was a direct replacement for someone who had left the post, HR insisted any new hire meet the old criteria. The manager ultimately capitulated since he stood to lose the position completely if he did not agree to the specifications provided by HR.

Ironically, HR was running a course that same week encouraging managers to "think out of the box" and advertising the course with a quote from Gautama Buddha: "What we think, we become." In my opinion, HR should have added: "When we don't think, we become the same." Reading the course announcement from HR and then learning what happened to this particular manager gave us all a great howl (remember: laughing is good for you!).

As far as meeting preset standards are concerned, I can only relate this to my world. Not all HEFS and dog events involve Conformation. Some dogs may not meet the breed standard but have other talents other than just looking good. There are a wide variety of events at which dogs can win prizes and many of these events allow the dog to accumulate points toward a championship title. Such events include agility courses, obedience testing, barn hunting, herding, dock diving, and many more. Most events involve just an individual dog, but quite a few are team events, such as dog sledding and Flyball. Believe it or not, there are even Dog Olympics!

Reign, who is a Grand Champion in Conformation, often teases me that I'm clearly not as good looking as she since I am not a champion. Pam and Barry just wanted me for their loving pet, and so certain vital parts of my anatomy were removed when I was young, thus excluding me from competing. I was never really given a fair chance! I counter Reign by pointing out I passed both my CGC (Canine Good Citizen) and Therapy Dog tests—on the same day! Reign also passed her CGC test—but I told her that Therapy Dog tests are *really* tough! Only "special" dogs (like me) merit a passing grade!

I've already mentioned that Barry likes sports, and I've heard him talk about how poorly his birth country often performs at football (soccer). He claims the reason for this is because some of the team managers choose only the country's most-talented players. Barry calls these players "a bunch of prima donnas who could not score a goal together if their lives depended on it." In England, soccer is regarded very seriously, so what most of the soccer stars failed to realize is that their lives were probably on the line! The individuals concerned were too dense to understand the danger! The point he was making, I believe, is that taking the best people and just throwing them together does not necessarily give you the best result.

To illustrate my point: Dogs that pull a sled are called a "dog team," not "a bunch of wonderful canines that make the sled move." The sled driver usually chooses and places each dog in the team according to various complementary strengths. I found the following comment from a sledding enthusiast on the internet: "Putting together a dog sled team may sound as easy as buying a few trained sled dogs—but, in all actuality, putting together a team that can work together takes an incredible amount of time and effort. You can't just pick a handful of dogs and throw them together and expect them to gel into a highly trained dog sled team. A dog sled team is composed of all different types of dogs, with different strengths and weaknesses, and you need to identify those before you try to put your team together." The article goes on to point out that one dog must be the leader—and that the pack cannot function well without a strong leader.

Perhaps this article might be a good pointer (I'm a pointer, so I know about these things) about how to put a team together in a company? I suggested to Barry that he should write a letter to the latest England team football manager and include the dog sled excerpt. Barry went red in the face and came out with words that I neither understood nor had heard before! Then Pam entered the room and she told him to cease swearing (I assume this refers to the new words with which I was unfamiliar) and to stop acting like a little child. He calmed down but sulked in his chair for the next hour or so. Barry is a pretty mild sort of guy, so his display was completely out-of-character. I can only conclude that many of the former football players representing England were nearer to death than they had realized.

Specific job descriptions can become a little fuzzy and more general in nature at smaller companies because individual specialists are expensive. Smaller companies are often looking for people with basic skills in core functions. Such employees are often chosen for their willingness and enthusiasm to learn and cover other jobs that may have to be completed, even though such jobs sometimes may be considered "menial."

In such successful smaller companies, if a team member has an area of weakness, or just dislikes performing a particular function, there always seems to be some other colleague who has the skill in question or has always wanted to try that job but was never given the opportunity to "give it a go."

As an example, Barry was grumbling one day about having to muck out the horse stalls. To his astonishment, both Pam and her friend said they would be more than happy to do the job because they really liked mucking out. They found it therapeutic.

Barry was amazed that anyone could find cleaning up poop to be therapeutic and enjoyable, so he started asking other people at the barn how they felt about this. He was totally floored when he found that the majority of the ladies enjoyed the job—although he was relieved to discover most of the men were far less enamored. I remember Barry walking out of the barn, shaking his head and mumbling "it takes all sorts" and that he would "never understand women." I guess the moral of this story is never assume that because you find a job to be a chore that it might not be fun for someone else.

Functions that require very specialized knowledge that may not be core to the company's activities, such as legal, real estate, or finance, are often farmed out to an outside specialty agency. Even some larger corporations prefer to use advisors in areas such as human resources, insurance, and health and safety. It can be difficult for anyone other than a full-time specialist to be abreast of areas where statutes and laws are constantly changing. My thought is that the best leaders and managers should look outside the company if a skill or expertise is not available inside the company.

Be aware that team balance might need some adjustment when a new member is brought into an existing team or herd. Merlin was explaining to me that sensible humans will put a potential new member of a domesticated herd into an adjoining field. First, the humans can check on the health of the new animal to confirm no diseases are spread to the herd. Second, and just as important, the herd can introduce themselves over the fence to the new guy or girl. This process leads to a much greater acceptance rate of the new horse within the herd! Running a strange horse straight into a field occupied by an established herd can be dangerous for all concerned. Such a strategy can result in hoof and bite fights—and sometimes the damage is serious and cannot be undone.

Barry believes that if new members of human staff are thrown straight into a herd of humans without some prior introductions then readjustments will be necessary before the herd can settle down again. Humans may not bite or kick the new man or woman (although some might)—but fur can still fly if the existing team takes a dislike to the new member. I always advise gentle introductions. Why not use the interview process to allow existing staff to "nose over the fence," so to speak, and to be part of the decision-making process? This strategy can ease tensions later.

Some other thoughts about team member selection: Try to engage in a relaxed interview. Give each candidate adequate time to "make their case"—but don't prolong the discussions if the candidate has no hope of selection. Be honest. Don't shy away from telling a candidate he or she is not right for the job. Most will understand and appreciate your honesty.

In addition, respect your candidate by always ensuring they receive a formal notification as to whether they have been successful or not. Try to relay information to the candidate as soon after the interview as possible. Treat people as you would want to be treated. There is nothing worse than waiting for a letter that never comes. Who knows: Perhaps one day a candidate you are interviewing could be your new boss!

I am also often curious about employee evaluations. Evaluations were always a sore subject with Barry—and I think I understand why. I know from overhearing Barry that there are many different evaluation standards and that each company applies a selected evaluation metric for their own purposes. The evaluations are intended to: a) let the employee know how well their employer perceives they are performing to the standard; b) review the employee's job description for accuracy; c) make the employee aware of areas for improvement; d) offer the employee advice on training opportunities that will improve their skills and increase their career advancement prospects; e) allow for agreement between employer and employee on future measurable objectives; and f) give the employee the opportunity to discuss with their supervisor any areas of concern.

Barry was always a great proponent of properly adjudicated evaluations. He claims, however, that many of the systems were often abused. For example, sometimes the reviewer lost the plot in terms of the purpose of the evaluation. In larger organizations, where only limited training on the evaluation program is provided to employees and reviewers, a lack of consistency in the administration of the evaluations can often result in damaged morale.

All too often, supervisors or managers perform a once-a-year review in which stored-up grievances are aired. Many supervisors regard these evaluations as a means of "laying down the law." This lowly and shy canine believes there should be no surprises in these reviews. The evaluations should be a confirmation and summary of conversations that occurred throughout the year. In addition, the employee should not be surprising the employer—and should offer feedback when appropriate throughout the year. Both parties—employer and employee—bear responsibility to discuss issues as soon as they occur. Minor issues become major dustups if left to simmer.

Many reviewers take it upon themselves to attempt to identify an individual's weaknesses—and to then spend company time and effort in shoring up these weaknesses. The reviewer might send the candidate to training classes, or give them measurable performance criteria to meet, and then review progress at their discretion to ensure improvements are made.

My fur stands on end when I think about this strategy—for this just puts people back in a box. Reviews focused only on weaknesses are unsettling—and employees will inevitably grow to dislike their jobs if forced to concentrate only on their weaknesses.

By the way: Evaluations should be a time for the supervisor to assess his or her own performance, too. Supervisors should encourage a subordinate to discuss any areas where they feel supervision can be more effective. In my opinion, no one should leave an evaluation feeling depressed, frustrated, or angry.

Cesar Millan once said: "I'm open for possibilities. I'm open for choices. I always welcome new ideas. I'm always eager to learn. I'm never going to close my mind from learning." Cesar always said he learns so much from dogs. Perhaps it's best not to think of your employee as a dog, but don't be afraid to learn about yourself from the people who work for you. After all, your success is largely tied to how they feel about you and your ability to guide them.

We dogs and horses have found that you will succeed if you love what you are doing. If we don't like doing something? Then we just don't do it! Simple but effective—although this can irritate our human companions! In a pack or herd, we focus on strengths and choose the animals best suited to perform particular functions. This is important for the safety and wellbeing of the group. If humans are prepared to listen, perhaps there is yet another lesson here that they could learn from their four-legged friends.

I mentioned before that Barry likes sport and is a huge tennis fan. He was watching two male singles players going hammer and tongs in an open tournament in Florida. A commentator remarked about the amazing improvement in one of the players compared to the previous season. The player's world ranking had improved by nearly 60 positions and he was holding his own against one of the top 10 players in the world. The commentator wondered what had caused such a dramatic improvement. The co-commentator simply said, "He changed his coach," to which the other responded, "Ah, now I understand, and the new coach has been improving all of his weakness, right?" "Oh no," was the reply, "by further developing his strengths. They work on weaknesses, of course, but spend most of the time improving strengths."

The player in question was very fast around the court and had an amazing forehand—but tended to get caught off balance on his backhand. Previous coaches had concentrated on improving his backhand, a shot the player disliked. The previous coaches encouraged the player to hit more backhands to show his opponents he had mastered the stroke. The new coach, recognized as one of the top in his profession, taught the player to run around his backhand without exposing too much of the court to his opposition. The player was urged by his latest coach to take more shots on his strong forehand—and the player started to win more matches. His confidence and ranking steadily improved. In a pre-match interview, the player said he had never enjoyed himself so much on a tennis court.

How often does your coach at work encourage you to improve on your strengths? Does your boss just concentrate on your weaknesses? How do you feel about that? You might not be able to influence how your boss or supervisor treats you, but you do control how you treat others. Did a dog once bite you? This does not mean you should avoid petting or encouraging all other dogs. Feel free to pet and love on me at any time. (Just so you know: I'm authorized to receive treats at any time.)

We all need to be aware of our weaknesses—but not at the expense of playing to our strengths. Never feel intimidated or ashamed to love and be passionate about what you do. As Barry once said about one of the managers who worked for him: "He's extremely enthusiastic and gives 110 percent of himself all the time. He regularly does all the wrong things for all the wrong reasons but his devotion and love for the job carries him through to the right result." Barry also remarked about a manager working for another company: "He does all the right things for all the right reasons—but rarely gets the right result because of his lack of commitment."

The D.E.V. from this most humble and contrite but cuddly canine: Appreciate and evaluate your team and your resources before engaging in significant change. Sometimes simply shuffling the deck and reassigning tasks is all that is needed. If you do look outside the company, don't shy away from selecting new people who may be difficult to manage but who can bring new talents into the team.

Using guidelines or standards is a sensible strategy—but don't be afraid to use common sense and gut instinct when selecting someone to join the team. Be flexible if an outstanding candidate is available that may not meet all the requirements in the "standard" (job description). Avoid getting "boxed in" by the organizational chart and job description.

Treat every candidate with respect. Listen to what they have to say. Search for other skills that may be outside of the immediate requirements. Tell a candidate immediately if he or she does not fit your team. Always let unsuccessful candidates know as soon as possible.

Actively bring other members of your team into the interview discussions so that you can observe interactions among the parties; in other words: "Let the dogs see the rabbit." Dogs like seeing rabbits! Some team members may take a nip or two—but better in the interview process before a decision is made to hire!

Bring energy and enthusiasm to your job. Understand your weaknesses but trade on your strengths. Look for enthusiasm and commitment from candidates who truly want to join your team. Search for weaknesses but understand all of the strengths and benefits that a potential member can bring to your existing team.

Use reviews or evaluations as a means of connecting with your subordinates and superiors to confirm and summarize points of discussion that have occurred throughout the year. Use reviews to offer an opportunity for open and two-way discussion, to identify and provide skill enhancement opportunities, and to set clear objectives. Ensure that people who work for you walk out of reviews rejuvenated and enthusiastic.

May the horse be with you!

THOUGHT EIGHT

Get That Bone!
~ *Strategy, Tactics, and Implementation*

The words "strategy" and "tactics" were originally military terms employed by humans to ensure they could be the winner when at war. In most cases, there can only be one winner in a war. No doubt both sides believe they have right on their side—but when one side lacks conviction about their cause they often lose. Odd creatures, humans.

I'm not sure that animals have "strategies" in the same way as humans running a business. An animal's major strategy is just to successfully survive! Animals know instinctively that adaptation to circumstances is critically important. Perhaps human businesses shouldn't be so far off from animal strategies?

Many employees do not know, or do not care, about their company's long-term plans—but I believe employees *should* care. Understanding where the company is going—or trying to go—and how and why can affect both the way you think about the company and the contribution you believe you can make toward success. Knowing more about the company can also help you to decide whether you want to stay—because the best time to look for a job is when you don't need to!

Most businesses have two types of plans: strategic and tactical (or operational). Each plan serves a different purpose but both have similar goals: to help the company survive and thrive. Each plan has elements similar to the other but are expressed over different timelines and, of course, with different details.

A strategic plan looks at the Big Picture and provides a blueprint for the business. I have heard humans use blueprint to mean "guide," although I understand the word originally meant a blue photographic image of a plan or technical drawing. I must admit: I like the word "blueprint" as blue happens to be one of my favorite colors.

A strategic plan usually describes what the business is, what market or customer set is addressed, how the business will meet a particular need over a longer period of time, who the competitors are, what barriers of entry exist to that market (if any), what skills or special qualities the business needs (or already owns) to succeed in that market, approximately what investments are needed, what resources and expenses are required to support the business in the future, and what differentiates the business from its competitors. Three-, five-, seven-, or even 10-year plans are not uncommon.

Most strategic plans focus more on direction and endgame rather than detailed financial planning. In-depth financial planning is presented in the short-term, tactical plan, which typically reflects activities for the next financial year. The longer the term of the strategic plan the less based in reality it becomes, as so many external factors can influence its direction. For example, today's fast-moving technologies and economies make market predictions increasingly difficult. Technological advances occur so frequently that companies often don't know which way to turn—but one thing this dog knows: Those that stick doggedly (pun intended) to their original strategies when change is necessary will suffer, fade, or completely disappear.

This four-legged advisor believes it is essential for companies to build flexibility into strategic plans. An extremely detailed strategic plan becomes rigid. When change should be incorporated, there is often a reluctance to abandon the many hours of work that were needed to develop the detailed plan. Companies must treat these plans as guides and not concrete directives. I know that I will try many paths to procure a bone—but I move on if, over a reasonable time, I am unable to score a bone, particularly if circumstances have changed. Dog owners: Watch your pet! A dog will simply wander off and pursue a new activity when an objective simply cannot be reached. Remember the quote Einstein is credited as saying: "The definition of insanity is doing the same thing over and over again and expecting different results."

When economies falter, or at least begin to decline, most humans sigh heavily, prepare to tighten their belts, and feed us dogs and horses' cheaper food. I hate economic downturns. Both the quality and quantity of food drops, treats are harder to come by, and humans are grumpier. In recent times we have seen many well-known companies downsize dramatically or even go out of business. I bet those companies weren't flexible or nimble! (I am very nimble and can always jump high for a treat!) Companies must always test their plans against different scenarios. Does your company have a "Plan B" and "Plan C"? I hope so—because actions taken in haste and under pressure (Barry calls them "knee-jerk reactions") almost never end well.

Barry expressed surprise during the last economic downturn that businesses he believed were robust and among the leaders in their field suddenly closed. One of them was a large bookstore chain that had a relatively new and large store not far from where we live. Barry grumbled about that one as he and Pam loved to visit the store, have a coffee and a slice of cake, and review magazines and publications. *Occasionally* they even bought a book—but I guess that was the problem. Like so many others, Pam and Barry had turned toward electronic media to both buy and read their books.

The chain of stores in this story had been very slow to react to the increasing public acceptance of electronic media sales. Books from internet competitors could be downloaded onto a suitable medium and at a lower expense. Cost and convenience matter!

Regrettably for the bricks and mortar book shops: Many folks would still visit the stores to find books that appealed to them—but would then return home to purchase the lower-cost electronic version from the latest digitally based supplier.

In addition: Don't forget to tell your managers and employees what you are trying to achieve. What are your personal strategic and tactical plans? I often have to listen to folks who visit our house where they complain that they are being led by mushroom management. At first, I thought they meant that their management had turned toward the food industry! These people said they were fed manure all day and never allowed to see the light of day. Enlightened and informed employees make for a much happier and well-motivated group. Remember: We all want to have more fun at work!

Let's look at an example of beneficial long-term planning. What might you think about when hiding a bone? I have had several unfortunate failures of late where I did not take sufficient time to think things through. I hid bones believing that Reign and I would be the sole canine occupants in the house. Reign has always been very respectful and only tries to steal clearly noticeable bones—but I now have to re-evaluate my plans. First, Katie appeared. A four-month-old, inquisitive, teething puppy will go to unbelievable lengths to satisfy the need to wrap teeth around a nice, succulent piece of bone—and Katie quickly found many of my hidden bones. Second, since Barry retired, he and Pam have started to discuss downsizing, which I discovered means living in a smaller house.

This all means I have to start thinking about the longer term. What is the intention for my bones in the future? Are these bones keepsakes? Are they emergency supplies stored for a rainy day? Will I want to dig them up one day and taunt the other dogs with the size and beauty of my prize possessions? Where, and how, do I store my remaining trophies? Do I want to add more bones to my collection? How quickly can I recover the bones if we move? How can I stop competitors from stealing my bones? What kind of bone protection can I expect or look for if we move?

All questions I should have asked myself long ago. Why did I not plan? That's a rough question! (Pun again intended!) Please do not hesitate to contact me with your ideas, solutions, or thoughts. My bone collection, or what's left of it, is very dear to my heart—and my stomach!

Here is an example in the human business world: Assume that the stated strategy for a business is to become the leader in a specific market by stealing market share from competitors using lower prices to win orders. Underpricing can often work well—but financial stability is paramount.

Many companies use a discounting strategy that includes low-operational costs and high efficiency. This is not, however, one of Barry's favorite strategies. He believes that the lowest price may be attractive to certain clientele but that this strategy is not always sustainable over the long term. The barrier of entry is almost non-existent should another competitor enter this market space by using their own low-cost model. In Barry's limited opinion, companies that survive over decades are those that deliver the best value or have differentiated themselves from the competition.

Do I dare mention Apple? I like thinking about Apple because Apple is a name you can eat—and I'm always hungry. Apple's strategic plan was brilliant: The company set itself apart from other tech companies by allowing users to easily link different Apple products, such as the Macintosh computer, iPhone, iPad, and iPod. Apple made synchronized tech simple! Barry laughed recently when he saw that the concept of integrated Apple products was referred to as "hardware and software fusing." He said that sounded like everything was about to blow a gasket! Barry's sense of humor is weird.

Barry often talks about how he always purchases Audis—even though he can't really afford them. He buys them because he loves Audis: He loves the overall style and quality of the car, the reliability and engineering—and because he enjoys playing with all the gizmos. His main reason for buying Audis? He loves the local dealer's outstanding service and support. Customer loyalty should be highly valued and never underestimated.

Barry always tells his friends and his wife that he believes Audis provide good value—even though Audis are usually more expensive when compared to other brands of cars offering similar, or even better, specifications. Barry is a bit quirky this way. He does not mind buying an expensive meal if the ambience of the restaurant is good, service outstanding, and the taste and standard of food exceptional. Yet both Pam and Barry hate spending money on any meal, even if it's really inexpensive, if the food is tasteless or of very low quality. I like this approach because Pam always chooses only the tastiest and healthiest food for us dogs and horses.

A tactical plan is a series of shorter-term events or actions that support the overall strategy. Animals use tactics all the time! Tactics allow us to adapt to new circumstances or even live more comfortably in our existing surroundings—and we always try to move if, for some reason beyond our control, we think we cannot meet our strategic objective of successful survival.

A tactical, or operational plan, typically looks at the upcoming business year and generally includes month-by-month details regarding areas such as expected revenue, project target dates, required resources, and subsequent results. The operational plan then becomes the standard by which success is measured.

Many companies provide quarterly results to public shareholders or private stakeholders and compare on-going results to the "one-year" operational plan. A forecast, or predicted expectation, for the rest of the term of the operational plan will most likely be offered together with an explanation behind current results and an estimated outlook measured over a moderate timeframe. Sometimes strategic initiatives or changes are also discussed.

Measurements for businesses are critically important. I've heard people say that what gets measured gets done or managed. I'm not entirely sure what this means except that I know it's a jolly good idea to keep score to know how you are doing—like when I play catch with my humans. The humans usually lose!

Unfortunately, some humans plan so much that opportunity passes them by. We animals say that a missed opportunity means we "missed the boat"—which I believe refers to certain animals who arrived too late to climb aboard the Ark. Smart competitors are quick to market and achieve a strong balance between planning and implementation. Success is a matter of urgency and good timing.

In addition, too often we see products or services ahead of their time brought to market by enterprising entrepreneurs. Humans, with a few notable exceptions, don't easily accept new ideas—and these new products and services often fail. Balance is critical: One mustn't wait too long—but, at the same, one's product (and plans for the product) must be well-developed and adequately promoted.

Even Steve Jobs faced strategic and tactical challenges when he introduced certain products. For example, check out the history of the iPad. Only through great persistence and patience—and by educating consumers through incremental steps about the product's advantages—did the iPad succeed.

What of actual implementation of your wonderful strategic and tactical plans? The jobs have to be done! Animals excel in implementation of plans. Our natural instinct is to always carry out our operational plans—because not doing so could mean the difference between life and death. Humans, on the other hand, often fail to recognize the importance of this part of the jigsaw puzzle.

Prompt implementation with commitment is necessary or the best results will not accrue. Barry often recounts stories about when he was working for a large corporation. There was one group who excelled at both strategic and tactical planning—but the group frequently failed to implement the plans they had so carefully constructed. This group was comprised of extremely bright people who left implementation to "the other guy." The group displayed no sense of urgency, no commitment, no ownership of their work, and, above all, no leadership. What happened? The group, for all their great ideas, did not succeed in successfully bringing products to market.

How do I plan? I'm glad you asked! Here is one example:

First: I develop my strategic objective: "Owning another dog's bone by taking the bone with daring and cunning."

Second: I plan a series of maneuvers (tactics) that will allow me to lull the other dog into a false sense of security. I plan to create a diversion so that I can swoop in to steal the bone and then run off to a safe place

I then implement my plan—and I don't overplan!

Tactic one: I lay a little way off from the enemy—sorry, I mean the other dog. I know my limits because I watch for the other guy's lips to start curling up and his teeth to start showing. I call this tactic "The first warning."

I then roll over on my back—but I accidentally roll near to the bone. I call this the "Oops, did I get near your bone? Sorry!" tactic. The act of laying on my back is crucial, as all dog companions will tell you this is an act of submission. Sneaky, huh? The other guy accepts this act of submission and thinks he is naturally superior. Even dogs have egos.

Then I prick up my ears as if something is happening outside of our immediate space. That sure gets his attention! This is my brilliant "What the heck was that?" tactic.

Then, suddenly, I leap to my feet and begin to bark as aggressively as possible. This is the "Danger, Will Robinson!" tactic.

The other dog now believes something is going on that he cannot see but should be aware of—and he steps away from his bone to investigate. This is my special "Gotcha" tactic.

As soon as my competitor starts to investigate: My opportunity to implement the final tactic is here! I swoop in, take the bone, and run as fast as possible to a safe hiding place. I call this "The Bonehead Maneuver"!

Objective achieved!

All the elements are here: I have a decided strategy, or overall objective, which is owning the bone. I have developed a series of tactics that will give me the best chance of achieving my prime objective. I then implement my tactics through dogged cunning and superb canine timing. Hot diggity dog—I'm good!

Remember: Never leave implementation to chance. I cannot tell you how many times I have seen another dog try to copy my "Own-a-Bone™" plan: They state the objective, carefully work out their tactics—and then are then ever-so sloppy when they implement. The look of surprise on some of my friend's faces when their intended victim sees right through their plot is hilarious—but not so funny for the poor planner! Inferior planning in the dog world can lead to very painful consequences. Some dogs have no sense of humor—particularly where bones are concerned. Even the most docile dog can turn into a torrent of rage and hate if his or her bone is under siege.

The D.E.V.: Know what you want to achieve, decide the course you will take to reach your objective, and make sure you follow through with appropriate actions.

Write down your thoughts and hone them to become your strategic objective. Be clear, simple, and unambiguous in your strategy. Do not overcomplicate the strategy. Be succinct! As I always say: "Too many words spoil the bone!" Communicate the strategy throughout the organization and elsewhere. If everyone understands your strategy and direction, you will have achieved a major milestone for your business. Customers, employees, and investors will invariably provide support when they understand what you want to achieve and how you plan to reach your objectives.

Develop strong tactics in order to successfully achieve your goals. Be certain you have the appropriate resources in place to achieve your expected results. Implement your plans with care. Don't change plans just for the sake of change—but be prepared to be flexible if situations change. Do not work with plans that are outmoded, outdated, or when and where circumstances demand change. Don't underestimate the importance of good timing.

Most of all: Beware of the big dog—and stay out of the reach of his teeth!

Thought Nine

Please Don't Bite Me!
~ *Respect*

Being the good boy I am, I looked up the *Oxford English Dictionary* definition of "respect": "A feeling of deep admiration for someone or something elicited by their abilities, qualities, or achievements." For me, respect means many things and includes many emotions.

In the animal world, respect for another animal or a situation can be the difference between life and death. I'm not sure I admire the Rottweiler who lives two streets away, but I certainly respect that he's capable of taking me down in a heartbeat—and I don't even need to sniff his bottom to understand that fact. I know that Barry does not admire someone called IRS, but he appears to have a deep respect for him. It appears that Barry doesn't have to sniff IRS's bottom either to know this guy is trouble. I assume, like the Rotty, IRS is big, aggressive, and capable of taking down Barry in a single bite.

Respect is an important element for success in life and business. I believe there are two types of respect. One type of respect is earned and then given over time through the experience of another's actions, attitudes, or leadership. The second type of respect, which is discussed later, relates to when respect is given, expected, or demanded because of social, hierarchical, or business position.

Earned respect is often the most treasured. Admiration often coincides with a fondness or even love for a person or an animal. Many of us would like to try to mimic some of the qualities shown by an individual we admire. However: We don't need to like someone in order to respect them. I have often disliked a particular dog or animal but I have respect for who or what they are.

I have lived with cats for most of my life and I cannot say that any of them have been my best buddies. I prefer those that run away when I chase them—as I am the bigger and more aggressive master of all that I survey. I never catch the cats. I let them think they are faster than me because I'm just a big-hearted softy. Yes: That's my story and I'm sticking to it.

Some years ago, I lived with a cat named Sasha. She was beautiful, part Siamese, with soft silky hair and eyes that looked right through you. Sasha also had a very high-pitched screech that would set my teeth on edge when she wanted something—usually her food. Whenever I approached, Sasha would stand her ground and wave a sharp paw at me. I found this action intolerable and disrespectful—but I respected her bravery once I tasted her sharp claws. I soon gave up trying to scare her off—much to the amusement of Pam and Barry—although I will never forget the feeling of humiliation.

The other dog I was living with at that time, Domino, used to look up from her bone and snicker. Domino was part Boston Terrier, part something else. I was just a puppy but Domino had lived with this cat for many years, well before I arrived on the scene. Domino knew exactly what to expect. Domino fell short of outright laughing at me and she was at least decent enough to suppress her desire to howl out loud.

I was fond of Domino and respected her for all she taught me. She was a very smart dog and I would often follow her example, particularly in the area of problem solving. She was able to confound humans on almost every occasion.

For example, Domino had an instinct for when toenail clippers were about to be used. On one occasion she crept quietly into a corner in such a way that Pam and Barry could not get at her. The cunning humans, however, knew that Domino could easily be tempted by food—so they laid a trail of treats to where they wanted to clip her toenails. At the end of the trail? A big and juicy reward of a piece of meat. The idea was that they would swoop in and snatch her as Domino grabbed the prize.

Domino, however, was smarter than any mere human. She followed the trail right to the big reward and, just when the humans were licking their lips with anticipation, Domino suddenly turned and took off at great speed back toward her corner. Pam and Barry wailed in despair and, stupidly, started to chase after her. Domino, of course, had everything figured out. She knew the treat path led into a hallway with another door that opened up into the room with the big treat. All she had to do was hit the door, run into the room, grab the reward, and keep on running back around to her hidey-hole—and, with the humans in hot pursuit behind her, this is exactly what she did.

Pam and Barry threw their arms into the air in a gesture of defeat, shook their heads in disbelief—and then started laughing. They had come to respect Domino's intelligence and problem-solving ability and knew anger would do them no good. Although Pam and Barry would eventually develop tactics that would allow them to clip Domino's toes, I knew they admired, respected, and loved Domino for her smarts. I would often hear them brag to their friends about her. If nothing else, Domino provided great tales (or should that be tails?) to tell when friends came to visit.

Barry has often said that he was very blessed in his long working career to have worked for bosses that he both deeply admired and respected. Barry did not always admire how some of these bosses treated other employees—but Barry admired how *clever* they were and he learned a great deal from them about how to run a successful business. Barry often had to determine the motivations behind some decisions and how he could add value—but, in time, mutual respect and trust was established. As I've already mentioned: Trust is essential when coaxing the best performance from a team. Barry found working with these folks delightful once the bonds were in place and communications were easy and unambiguous.

Now let's talk about the second type of respect. There are always people we don't respect—but without respect the chances of *working* successfully with someone is reduced significantly. If trouble arises—and mutual respect is absent—you might want to consider a change before a change is made for you.

Not every leader or superior will command the respect of his or her troops. Barry learned this lesson late in his career—much to his disappointment and surprise. Barry learned that if you do not respect another individual then you will not be able to trust them—and communications can go badly awry. Why do things in business go wrong? Situations can be complex and problems are not always the result of a single event or circumstance. Here is what I know: You will not like everyone you meet and they may not like you—and you may never even know why—even if you have sniffed their bottom.

Respect can be given because of position or status if merited. For example, I can respect the pack leader because of his or her position, for in the animal world the head of the pack typically has performed some act that has earned them the right to be the leader. The leader may have earned his or her position because of great wisdom or outstanding fighting ability. When respect is expected or demanded because of position—and nothing else—I prefer the word "deference." For me, "respect" implies that an individual has values that appeal to me.

If I understand the principles of business, then respect is required for the "boss"—the one to whom everyone reports. I have listened to the discussions of some folks who have visited our house—and I know that not everyone respects their boss. When people don't respect their boss, however, they have often learned to "defer" to the boss—since decision-making responsibility rests at the top. Some workers defer to their boss because they are afraid of losing their job or because the boss is a bully. My observation: Trouble is afoot when people defer rather than respect their boss.

Some positions automatically carry the mark of respect. For example, in England, Barry's homeland, the Monarchy wields little power, but is, in general, respected by the populace. The Monarchy is viewed as an ambassador or proud representative for England and its values. Barry has pointed out that the Monarchy has often fought through troubled times with a "stiff upper lip." Why anyone would want a stiff upper lip is beyond my comprehension! How can one bark, eat, or drink unless your lips are loose?

In general, animals tend to respect those who prove themselves worthy. In most herds, packs, flocks, or whatever the collective name might be, respect is given to the chosen or accepted leader. Not every animal in the group will respect the leader, however, and that is often when trouble starts or leadership changes. Unlike in the human world, though, an animal will not respect another animal simply because the other animal was brought up in better circumstances.

For example, I am a true-blue thoroughbred—whereas Domino was a mixed breed—but ancestry means nothing in the animal kingdom and does not translate into higher social standing. Animals are so much healthier in this respect (no pun intended) than humans, don't you think?

Voluntary change may not always occur in the human business world if an individual, or even a group, does not respect either their immediate superior or folks higher up the chain. There may be nothing an individual or group can do to make change happen, in which case the only solution is to move away from that situation to something else. Often this is easier to say than to do for many reasons—but the misery that can accompany putting up with the lack of respect for another can lead to depression, anger, or even illness. A bad working environment can often affect relationships with colleagues, friends, or loved ones. Sometimes one must take decisive action—and without regret.

Before we leave the subject of respect, just a couple of additional thoughts from this handsome, playful, wonderfully modest canine. I attended a horse dressage clinic recently with Pam and Barry. A 70-plus-year-old ex-Olympian led the clinic. The woman displayed extraordinary knowledge and amazing training skills—and she commanded the respect of every horse and rider. I know this because I talked with the horses once they were put back in their stables.

This lady commanded respect not just because she was the leader of the seminar or because the riders trusted her knowledge—but because *she* respected the participants and, as a result, the participants respected her. Everyone—novice and advanced riders alike—learned so much! I was humbled by her skills.

Sometimes we all, humans and animals alike (but mainly humans), fail to appreciate, and thus respect, those around us. We all get caught up in our busy lives of eating, sleeping, working, and playing—and whatever else humans do! It is all too easy to ignore others who should be given our respect for what they do every day of our lives, no matter how menial the task might seem to us. I know I shall be trying to do a better job in the future just by staying aware of what others are doing for me. For example, when Pam and Barry pick up all our toys, Katie, Reign, and I delight in getting every single one out of our box to play! It's such wonderful fun to clutter up the house again—but I also know that the toys would be mislaid or even damaged if Pam and Barry did not tidy them up. I respect Pam and Barry for cleaning up the toys each time—even though they know they are fighting a losing battle against us Vizslateers.

Pam often remarks that if the trash company (Barry calls them the "dustmen"—another term from the old country) did not pick up all of our rubbish each week, our housing estate would be less than a pleasant place to live! The British respect their "dustmen." There is even a song, recorded in 1961 by Lonnie Donegan dedicated to dustmen, called "My Old Man's a Dustman." It's very catchy and can be found on YouTube.

Wouldn't it be great if puppies and human children could learn to have more respect for their parents and elders? Later in life they will discover that all their parents were trying to do was to look out for the health and welfare of their offspring. I have learned to appreciate and respect what my parents tried to do for me—even though at the time I felt they were restricting my freedom.

I know humans feel the same way! When the kids talk to Pam and Barry (hardly "kids" anymore given that one is 42 and the other 39), I often hear them remark that now that they are older, they understand why their parents took certain actions, or why the parents acted the way they did. Daughter is especially understanding now that she has two children of her own. Another act of respect, perhaps, is to realize how things might look from the other person's point of view. I try to do this all the time, particularly as I consider how things might be from a human perspective.

Humans: The poor darlings have so many disadvantages. First, humans only have two feet. It's a miracle to me that they manage to balance at all, and of no surprise to me how often they fall over. Second, humans get caught up in so many emotional things they hardly know what day of the week it is. Most of them try not to let their emotions show—so how do you know what they are thinking? Third, the majority of humans are so self-focused that they can only think of themselves to the exclusion of all around them. Maybe that is why they try to hide their emotions?

Dogs and horses are more obvious and simple with their emotions. They are happy, sad, angry, frustrated, hungry, or in pain. Of course, I *have* known horses that hate to show when they have problems. Sometimes, when Pam is working her therapy magic, some horses will try not let on when she reaches some of their tender spots. To hide their anxiety, we have seen horses bury their heads in an empty bucket, or under a blanket, rather than let Pam see she has reached a problem area. Many animals accept pain, discomfort, disability, or injury as a part of life—think about how you may have seen a three-legged dog running around as though it had not a problem in the world—unlike humans who immediately swallow lots of pills and retire to their beds moaning and groaning.

The D.E.V.? Respect is extremely important in our day-to-day interactions. Earning and giving of respect helps us grow, leads to wonderful relationships, and helps us to learn and recognize opportunities. Respect leads to trust—and trust is an essential ingredient for friendship, relationships, and successful leadership.

Be aware that respect given because of another's skills or position can be acceptable, but respect given through fear is merely an illusion. History repeatedly shows that fear-based respect does not last forever. Eventually action will take place to replace those who govern only because others fear them. Make sure you avoid garnering respect through fear.

Talking about changing a situation can often be easier to advise than to achieve because of individual circumstances. That said, if respect is missing in any kind of relationship just know that change will happen at some time, whether initiated by you or forced upon you.

We can, and should, respect others for what they do or what they are—no matter their position or job. We can respect others, even when we might not necessarily like them or agree with them. We can all do a better job of learning to respect others just by being more aware of what others can or have achieved. There is a reason why letters written to an individual are often signed off with "Respectfully Yours," as this phrase shows esteem by the writer to the recipient.

By the way, just to let you know, you can earn a great deal of respect from me by giving me a nice juicy bone.

THOUGHT TEN

My Bones Are Aching For Bones
~ *Payment Systems*

We all need bones and food to survive. My people need that funny money stuff in order to provide me, the other Vizslateers, and Merlin with our daily repasts, treats, and health requirements. We are happy to provide our humans with encouragement to earn their daily bread howsoever they can by cuddling and allowing them to rest with us. We like to feel we are contributing to the household budget and earning our living as part of the family.

Lavishing praise, offering treats, and providing some way to earn a crust (an English expression meaning to earn a living; Barry's sayings are rubbing off on me) are excellent ways to provide reward for good behavior or for when tasks are accomplished—but payment systems require structure or rules. Dogs and horses are just like puppies and human children: They will push the boundaries of acceptable behavior to the extreme until they understand the boundaries. My instructor told Pam and Barry that it is important to reward or scold us animals quickly after an event; otherwise we cannot make the connection between the event and the praise or censure. I suppose this is important. Does this rule apply to human behavior, too?

Barry believes that many employees and managers need to learn how to set and understand boundaries. He said he has problems setting boundaries himself—but, then again, he is of British stock, so explaining things in a way that makes any sense to people in the United States is difficult for him. Pam often recounts a time when she told Barry he needed to let another Brit know he was upset with their actions. Barry spoke to this individual while in Pam's ear shot, but in Pam's opinion he said very little and she could not see any way the other guy would have a clue that Barry was not happy. Later that day, the individual concerned sidled up to Pam and said, "Wow, Barry was really upset, wasn't he?" Pam's jaw dropped and all she could say was, "You understood he was mad with you?" "Oh, yes," was the response. "Barry rarely gets as annoyed as that." Pam was last seen wandering off mumbling, "Unbelievable. Absolutely unbelievable." That's the Brits for you!

Boundaries are important if some sort of discipline is to be maintained. Of course, I have my normal digital canine opinion on this subject, or "dog bytes," as I like to call them.

The military embodies strict boundaries and discipline. For an effective fighting unit to act as one cohesive body, accepting the boundaries and following the discipline of training can be a matter of life and death. The ability to survive is a reward all in itself! In animal training, however, as in human business, flexibility within the rules allows individuality to shine—sometimes with spectacular results.

Within these pages I have pointed out many times how successful animal trainers recognize that flexible discipline is best. The top trainers cater to an animal's character, strengths, and weaknesses. I have never seen a reputable horse trainer, for example, walk straight up to a horse, jump into the saddle, and start training. Some trainers will spend time examining the horse on the ground, often running their hands over the horse's body to get a feel for muscle tone or to look for problem areas. Without exception, however, they will all walk the horse around before beginning any other exercise to warm up their mounts and to gauge the strengths and weaknesses of the animal. Only after a trainer has a good idea about the condition of the horse will he or she decide on the best training exercises.

Tangible rewards are beneficial when re-enforcing and recognizing exceptional behavior. In the business world, rewards come in many forms. One type of reward is called salary or wage. Salary, I'm told, is a regular payment for non-manual work, while a wage is money paid for labor or services. Either way, many people seem to believe they are underpaid, or that they are not paid an equal or fair amount when compared to someone else. Fortunately, animals are only interested in eating, having fun, and being themselves, so the worry about how to earn more money is of no concern to them. Our regular food and treats, on the other hand, are a whole different plate of beans (or tasty liver snacks)!

Other types of business rewards include monetary incentives (such as bonuses, commissions, shares in the company, and so forth), or even non-monetary incentives such as additional benefits, free meals, gifts, vacations, and so on.

I do know that, no matter how one receives a reward, the big and scary dog called IRS (pronounced ERRSS, I believe) gets a share of everything. Everything! I've heard Barry call this "taxation." I know I would feel "taxed" if I had to hand over a part of every bone to ERRSS! Somebody told me that there is an equivalent of this big ERRSS guy in just about every country in the world!

Be aware that a non-monetary benefit will likely also carry a value that is ascribed to it by dogs like ERRSS. From what I've learned, ERRSS and the other big dogs require they be given their "fair" share of any reward! According to Barry, ERRSS will ensure you are severely punished if you don't pay up and on time. My guess is that ERRSS and his friends will take a big bite out of your bottom if you do not happily part with the crispy ones. I know Pam and Barry have to write down stuff and send papers to ERRSS so he knows exactly what rewards Pam and Barry have received and how much they will need to pay him. I can only conclude that ERRSS is even bigger and fiercer than a Doberman with lots of sharp teeth. I admit I do not have a record of all the bones I have received over the years!

For some humans, the monetary-based reward system can take over their lives. For example, I know employees can grow angry and become disruptive if they believe they are not receiving adequate rewards. There will always be employees who constantly seek financial equity with others—even when additional rewards are not merited. Others will seek to push the system as far as it will stretch—just to gauge their worth. There will also always be employees who feel they deserve more—no matter how many rewards they receive.

Most companies try to achieve compensation systems that are reasonably fair—but payment structures often depend on employee attitudes, the financial situation of the company, and particular approaches and policies of the company. Some employees judge their satisfaction at work by how much money they are paid—and I think these folks will never be happy. Barry always referred to these types of employees as "a ticking time bomb," since eventually one day they will explode.

What is a good or fair monetary reward? As always, this boy can only see from the canine perspective—or "the hangdog look." If I am rewarded for work I perform for my companion, then I must decide if my reward is acceptable and meets my needs. I cannot deny I look to see what my friends are getting—as I expect nothing less! Sometimes, as when we are playing, I accept less because I enjoy the work—although I do try to avoid letting anybody take advantage of my fun-loving character. I know, though, that the facts are the facts: My companion decides the size and nature of the reward.

Merlin told me that he and his friends receive rewards in a similar way—but I understand there are differences between humans and animals. If Merlin or I do not receive the same treat as others, or no treat at all, we just accept the situation and move on. Sometimes we dogs might complain by whining, barking, or snorting—and I gather that my complaining, whining, barking, snorting approach is adopted by some humans. Further, I've heard rumors that there are humans who snarl and breathe fire from their noses if they feel the size of their reward is not adequate. Sounds ugly!

Unlike humans, however, we animals do not withdraw our labor if we feel under-compensated. Merlin told me that some horses, if not rewarded appropriately, will lose interest and may move on to other things. Even we dogs have been known to lose interest in a task if a reward is not forthcoming—but to completely withdraw our labor until we get what we want is not our "modus operandi."

Many corporations adopt a banding or grading system to determine compensation. These systems help to provide equitable hiring practices that promote diversity. A specific job is banded or graded according to its status, content, and responsibility level—and a basic salary or wage breakdown is determined. Employers often take into account the experience of an employee, years of service, past job performance, and/or geographical elements.

Another popular method for determining pay is called market pricing. This approach is customized by individual hire and is based on the fair market value for the employee. While flexible, market pricing sometimes opens up a company to discrimination lawsuits. Small businesses with few employees, for example, sometimes substitute a salary grade, or structured pay schedule, in order to document pay policies and avoid the awkwardness of reporting specific employee salaries.

From my lowly four-legged point of view: I believe that humans often need to surround themselves with legislation and rules in order to feel safe in their working world—but businesses often employ standards that are inflexible and restrictive. In such circumstances, how then does the company reward the best employees? Many companies offer bonuses, profit-sharing plans, and other systems to reward the most-outstanding performances. Some jobs (such as those in sales departments) offer commission plans, which I understand means performance-related earnings.

Another item worthy of mention: Many groups link salary and wage increases to performance reviews—and, of course, Barry has his own opinions about this issue. Barry believes that performance reviews and salary reviews should absolutely be delinked. He recognizes that a number of major CEOs advocate linking performance and salary reviews because this introduces an element of competition among workers—but Barry disagrees. Me? I never mess with the big dogs.

Even Barry admits linking performance and salary reviews may rest with the type of business. For example, when discussing performance-related menial and/or repetitive labor, and staff turnover is high, then linking reviews may be best. Barry believes that delinking is better for long-term strategies involving skilled employees. Company objectives, planning, and culture ultimately determine the best course of action.

Barry cites many reasons for maintaining a distance between performance and salary reviews. He lists a host of items that he firmly believes can affect the value of any job—some of which have nothing to do with individual employee performance. Included in this list is the regional worth of a job. For example, the scarcity or abundance of available candidates with appropriate job skills in certain areas can sometimes introduce an element of compensation competition. We three Vizslateers are honest, faithful souls, but I have to confess that when we are performing our tricks (they seem to amuse humans for some reason) even we often tend to turn to the person with the largest, or most tasty, treats.

Further, like shares on the stock exchanges, market worth for certain positions can rise and fall. Sometimes high-performing employees who have received consistent salary increases in recognition of past performance are paid more than they would be worth on the open market—and this can lead to employees feeling "trapped"—since they might be unable to change jobs without loss of earnings. Compensation certainly is a sticky wicket! Just give me my bones!

Salary increases are also sometimes limited by factors such as poor financial results. Employees are likely to not understand why they are not receiving a raise after a wonderful performance evaluation review when salary and performance reviews are linked—particularly if they have received increases in the past as a result of outstanding performance.

Barry also anticipates the following conundrum: What to do when a high-performing employee "tops out" (receives the maximum allowable rate for that function) in their job grade or banding? Many supervisors, faced with this situation, are reluctant to write a glowing report for fear that the employee expects a tangible increase in pay—and will be disappointed when the raise is not in line with past rewards. I know only too well that I bark my disapproval when I receive treats for outstanding performance and the rewards stop because my human companion feels I have "topped out" on those treats!

Timing is also an issue. Many companies review employees at the end of the fiscal and/or calendar year—often the period when supervisors, managers, and employees are all the most stressed. Salary and performance reviews add to the workload and the stress—and this almost inevitably leads to hastily completed reviews. Hurried salary reviews can be corrected easily; hurried and sometimes careless performance reviews can lead to major—and sometimes irreversible—damage.

How to avoid the many potential pitfalls associated with performance and salary reviews? Barry believes that both types of reviews should be viewed as opportunities.

Salary reviews can be used to discuss the value or market worth of a position and the general responsibilities and expectations of the job, such as trustworthiness, dependability, and consistency. New performance-related incentives and adjustments, such as profit-sharing and bonus plans, can be discussed. Barry believes performance reviews should occur before salary reviews because this gives an employee an opportunity to highlight value added to the company: Perhaps new responsibilities have been accepted, measurable productivity or performance have improved, or new skills have been added. Employees should never assume employers know everything about their jobs: As Barry is (overly) fond of saying: " 'Assume' makes an 'ass' out of 'u' and 'me.' "

First and foremost: Both parties should be talking to each other prior to a salary review so as to offer thoughts and ideas in a non-confrontational setting and manner.

Employees and employers are well-advised to do their research before salary reviews. I always advocate sharing salary information. There is plenty of salary information available on the internet covering a wide range of fields and jobs. I know I try to carefully track the number of bones received by Reign and Katie!

Barry believes every manager should receive training on how to read salary surveys. Unfortunately, many larger companies have a centralized Human Resources (HR) department that handles salary surveys—and, sadly, HR often has little or no direct contact with employees! Guidelines are sent to managers but a few HR departments are so far removed from everyday operations that it is unlikely they can understand individual situations.

Employers must be clear from the outset of the salary review. Employers should tell employees if decisions have already been made and no salary increase, or a smaller-than-usual increase, is the final decision. In addition, employers should discuss any restrictions that might affect the salary review, such as significant budget limits. constraints set by corporate dictate, or expense restrictions due to poor past financial performance. Of course, employees usually know what is going on within their company—because company grapevines often carry information faster than the internet! Barry used to hold an "all-hands" meetings once a quarter where he would discuss, if necessary, upcoming limitations on raises. Sharing financial details is wise!

When Barry started a company from "ground zero," there were only a few people to carry out the many jobs—and so everyone pitched in. Few of the generic job descriptions used in typical salary surveys or from employment agencies matched the daily tasks within the company. Still, as people were hired, Barry needed some rationale for the salaries he was offering. He hit upon the idea of estimating the split of time needed for various base functions. Each position carried with it an estimated percentage of time for the individual base function or task. Barry reviewed typical salaries offered by other local companies who could afford a full-time position for the various functions. The estimated salary for each specific function was then applied against the estimated percentage of time for each task. Finally, when each function had an assigned dollar value, the values were summed to give a final salary.

As the company grew, Barry, or the department manager, would sit with each employee at least once or twice a year and discuss the percentage of time spent against each of the tasks or functions—so that everything received a value that counted toward the final salary review. As salary reviews were held a minimum of once a year, specified times for reviews were less important. Salary raises were offered whenever an increase in responsibility occurred.

Employees were always encouraged to submit their own data for consideration if they felt that the company data was flawed. The system worked well for Barry, and employees generally accepted the principles of this arrangement as a reasonable way to calculate a salary value.

There is always more than one way to "skin a cat" when reviewing and determining salaries. Although "skin a cat" almost certainly originates from the use of the "cat o'nine tails" by the Royal Navy in olden days, and has nothing to do with cats, I am tempted by the idea of "skinning cats"—although I have to admit that skinning any animal is not a nice thing for the creature involved.

One last thought before we leave salaries and wages. Barry likes to talk about the concept of "total remuneration." He has seen employees leave to join another company because they were offered an increase in base salary or wage by the new employer—but they didn't really understand the financial implications of what they were leaving behind. For example, sometimes a new company might offer more in disposable income (weekly or monthly salary)—but the employee might actually end up with less money if he or she has to use the base salary increase to support individual services and benefits (such as health care or retirement plans) that were part of the total remuneration package in the original company.

I know friends of ours who left their company for the lure of a higher base salary—only to find that the grass on the other side was a lot less green than they expected. (Merlin says he can empathize with this because several times he has tried—painfully, when fence nails were involved—to reach greener grass—only to find the taste on the other side not worth the effort.) One friend learned his new base salary was higher but his new company did not offer any health benefits and the vacation allowance, often linked to length of service at the company, was considerably less. Our friend also learned too late that his new company did not offer a matched tax-advantaged retirement-saving plan, share options, or a profit-sharing program—all of which were in place at his old job. He really should have understood and confirmed the complete package before making his move.

Barry often asked independent financial advisors to talk to his employees. Some advisors will speak for free to company employees in the hopes of finding new clients. What are the best benefit choices for employees? Circumstances are different for everyone—so there is no best "cookie cutter" approach. In our kitchen I like to hear that a cookie cutter is being used since that often means scraps for me and the other Vizslateers.

When Barry worked in Europe, many moons ago, he received a nice company car every three to four years, complete with free maintenance, fuel, road tax, and insurance. He always considered this a wonderful gift. Needless to say, ERRSS's friend in the United Kingdom (HM Revenue & Customs—which is a crazy name for a big and scary dog!!!) felt he should be given an increasingly sizeable chunk of Barry's "gift." Barry didn't enjoy giving a large portion of his "gift" to HMR&C (Himarsee? That looks like a name you could have fun with!)—and so he wasn't that upset when he transferred to the company in the United States and was not offered a company car. Indeed, Barry was happy to be relieved of the financial burden.

Sometimes, even after discussions and negotiations for a higher salary, one must leave the job. Switching jobs is an individual choice—and many factors go into such decisions. This wise old dog, however, can offer this council: Always carefully review the complete package— perhaps with a trusted financial advisor—if financial considerations are driving your decision. Carefully research the new company, too! If you can, talk to current employees about the company. Do they like it? What do they like about it? And, perhaps most important: What *don't* they like about it? Talk to customers, too, if possible, about how they view the company.

If you must leave: Always try to leave on friendly terms and in good spirit. Never let frustration or anger boil over into a nasty conversation or malodorous note. Have you heard the phrase: "Don't burn your bridges"? The Romans would burn bridges once their troops had crossed a river to prevent the troops from retreating. The soldiers had no option but to fight for their lives. In modern business, however, where situations can change overnight (perhaps your new company might be acquired by your former employer), burning your bridges is never a smart option.

The quick D.E.V.: Where it is appropriate for the business, I suggest you separate salary reviews from performance evaluations. Be sure to assess and discuss performance with employees throughout the year. I strongly advise not to hold performance reviews during stressful periods when company focus is on other items, such as year-end shipments, holiday periods, or the end of the financial year.

Pam once made the point that you do not achieve the best performance or behavior from an animal by training, rewarding, or scolding once a year, or even at the end of a week. Continuous effort is required to coax and persuade any creature to give of it's best. Ask any parent! As a proud recipient of treats or praise resulting from my positive actions, I can assure you regular rewards for a job well done is the only way to go. Further, I soon learn which activities will bring the good stuff and which the reprimand. Performance that is assessed throughout the year will lead to continuous employee performance *and* satisfaction.

Use salary surveys as a way of comparing your own worth with similar positions in equivalent industries, but avoid "cherry picking" the parts of the surveys that you feel suit your best interests. While on the surface this might seem to be a great idea as a way of improving your monetary reward, if your manager understands and uses these surveys as a means of providing a fair recompense, he or she will be able to run a bus through the middle of your presentation. If you are a manager, make sure you understand how salary surveys operate and what they mean. In other words, make sure you "bone up" on the subject.

Should you decide to change jobs primarily because of perceived higher levels of reward, make sure you compare all factors to the total remuneration you currently receive. Remember that some less obvious tangible benefits, such as a subsidized health care scheme or a company-matched-savings plan, have a real monetary value. When offered a large, single, good-looking bone rather than a smaller but tastier specimen, I try to ensure my choice is a wise one. "Boneage," as I call it, is important. I always take advice from my friend, a French Poodle, about nutritional value when she wishes me "bone appetite."

As I always say, "A tasty bone a day helps you work, rest, and play."

THOUGHT ELEVEN

Treats, Treats, and Even More Treats
~ *Rewards Systems*

All of us enjoy rewards for good work or behavior. I like recognition for a job well done almost as much as the reward itself—and I wag my tail at a high speed to show my appreciation when I am praised—but I admit there is nothing more satisfying than a decent treat. There are few downsides to rewards—and there are many downsides to criticisms—particularly if the criticism is unjustified.

I remember when I first attended puppy class, too many moons ago to contemplate, the instructor was very clear on the issue of rewards. "Always praise or give a treat to your puppy when they do as they are asked." This was a wise lady—and I carry her advice in my heart and on my forepaw. I perfected the "poor me" look when I am not rewarded—and often Pam or Barry will give me a treat just because they think I look so pathetic. Whatever works!!!

In the human business world, offering treats to employees is an excellent way to show appreciation of a job well done—but I know that people need more than a full stomach of treats! After all, many people have bills to pay—or a desperate urge to buy things they don't really need!

How can an employer show appreciation, beyond salary or wage, for a job well done? We need an incentive plan! Barry claims that he has seen just about every flavor of incentive plan—some good but most that belong in the trash heap of history.

Barry believes that there are three elements in every plan that must be considered:

1. There are no totally, absolutely, completely fair plans.
There will always be unknown or unexpected events, real or perceived, that can scuttle the fairness factor. The gremlins are out to get you—and they will always win. Admit up front that your incentive plan is not 100 percent equitable—but that you have worked to make it as 100 percent reasonable as possible.

2. Some plans are too darn complex.
Overly complex plans benefit neither employer nor employee. The plan might not be in anyone's best interests if attorneys are needed to understand the fine print. In my sporting dog opinion, plans must contain some measurable—and easily understandable—parameters, such as the amount of product sold, the level of output, or company profit. Employees should be able to calculate results in real-time as the year unfolds.

In addition, some percentage of the total funds available—say 10 to 20 percent—should be left to a manager's discretion. Managers should be able to offer rewards to those who perform over and above the call of duty. Of course, one must always document the reasons for the additional reward or cries of favoritism will abound. Barry tells me he never had any problems in documenting examples of an individual's contribution to justify additional rewards.

3. Most plans are poorly written and communicated to employees.
When incentive plans are poorly drafted, they are often followed by the HR-penned "Explaining Memo." OMD! (That's "Oh My Dog!" By the way: The human word "god" is simply "dog" spelled backwards—and we know *she* is a big, scary, intelligent Great Dane. I know that some

humans are aware of the Great Dane: Only the other day, I overheard our garden guy mention to his fellow worker that he was "fed up with all this G.D. rain!") The "Explaining Memo" is meant to better describe the poorly written incentive plan—but management often forgets to explain the system to HR and so HR is left to its own devices. In isolation from the original management discussions, HR often leaves many questions unanswered—and, instead, creates chaos and confusion.

Barry oft relates the story of a company with one incentive plan for the financial department and another contradictory plan for the sales department. What fun! The managers from each department were often seen dealing with complaints from customers caught in the middle! I may be barking up the wrong tree (an old hunting expression used when dogs barked at a tree other than that utilized by the hunted animal—and yes, we all make mistakes, you know!) but I believe different departments within one company should be talking to one another and should circulate proposed plans for one and all to see and comment upon—before the plans are put in place for the employees!

Employees—those who stand to benefit most from the proposed plans—should be involved in the reviews of the plans, too. Barry has seen some of the best ideas for solid incentive plans come from employee suggestions.

Simple plans may not require a lot of explanation; complex plans always benefit from examples in order to illustrate the purpose and methodology behind the calculation of the measurement.

Incentive plans should include clear and achievable objectives within established timeframes. Why are the parameters important to the company? How do these parameters affect the company performance for all the interested stakeholders (including the workers)? Employees will perform at higher standards when they completely understand the company's goals and objectives. Overly complex plans are neither valuable nor sustainable—but neither are plans that are too simple!

How can plans be too simple? As an example: A salesperson is told that their incentive plan is based on sales growth over prior year. The salesperson, with no further guidance, in order to reach high sales growth, may offer larger discounts to the customer (if permitted to do so), try to offer preferential payment terms for the customer (which may not work well for the company if cash flow is an issue), or might offer some other enticement to persuade a customer to place an order.

If sales growth is achieved but the products are sold at a loss or in a way harmful to financial performance then this can hardly benefit the company (unless this tactic is part of a short-term strategic initiative to gain competitive advantage or for some other reason). Barry often refers to the old adage espoused by some that "what is lost on a single sale will be made up in volume." He says he has rarely seen the "volume" equation work—just the increases in losses multiply!

There are occasions when a company may use short-term discounts to sell a product or use a product as a "loss leader" in order to attract more profitable business at some later date. Short-term discounting is also sometimes used to gain a new presence in the market place or to steal market share from a competitor. Typically, however, these focused activities are not related to incentive plans and are, instead, time- or number-limited—and the result of some careful calculations that show profitable product sales expected in the relatively near-term.

Barry reckons that failure to describe the "what" and "why" of an incentive plan should alternatively be dubbed "The Company *Dis*incentive Plan." I cannot tell you how many times I've had to listen to tales of woe from friends at the dinner table as they recount the latest and greatest about the queue of people waiting outside of their office to complain about the introduction of a new company incentive plan.

Treats are great—but praise and recognition are extremely important for all of us. Recognizing someone through praise, giving someone a "pat on the back" (I prefer a nice petting session), presenting a prize or trophy (especially in a public forum) all go a long way to promoting a strong company culture—and give individuals a deep sense of satisfaction at work.

Unless a gift or monetary prize is on offer, recognition of a job well done costs very little—but can have a major effect on an employee's self-worth. We all love being told we are doing a good job! I know I do! I will do anything for praise—and I wag my tail furiously to show my appreciation!

Recognition of good work can be provided at the performance review—but letting people know how well they are doing is more effective if praise is offered throughout the year. Praise for work well done instills a strong sense of purpose, pride, and commitment to do even better. Recognition for specific tasks is more effective than general approbation.

Feedback of all sorts is important. Tell an employee sooner rather than later if you are not happy with his or her performance. For example, if an employee's performance (let's call him John) has been slowly deteriorating, you could say: "John, I've noticed you've been making some errors recently. Is there a reason for this? Can I help to get things back in track?"

If an employee isn't performing well, you may need to stop wagging your tail and show some teeth. Indeed, the employee may need to leave the pack. I believe in giving a dog every chance to show their worth—but there comes a point when their inability to add value to the pack has a deleterious effect on everyone. Never retain a poorly performing employee for too long. I have heard Barry lament several times that he failed to take appropriate action with an employee who either could not, or more likely would not, change their ways.

Barry used to present company results to his group once every quarter, recognize areas of both good and bad performance, set goals and objectives for the next quarter, and select individuals for special attention or praise as a way of recognizing strong performances. Whenever possible he would ask someone to represent their work or department and present the reasons why they believed they were doing well. These meetings communicated important information—and showed appreciation for great effort! Even when results are not going according to plan, let your staff know you have faith in them—because everyone performs at a higher standard when they take responsibility and ownership.

My D.E.V here is simple: Reward often and creatively. The proper forum for and presentation of praise and criticism is critical. Monetary and benefit rewards provide extraordinary positive reinforcement for top performance. Rewards presented in public forums are also very effective. Praise for a job well done is a strong form of reward, too.

Be sure to be clear and concise with any and all incentive plans. Avoid conflict among departments by ensuring plans are directed toward the same objectives. Don't overcomplicate plans.

Always keep a few bone treats in the larder for a rainy day. This has little to do with the rest of this chapter—but Tennessee has its fair share of rain and I believe in the Boy Scouts motto: "Be prepared." When asked, "Be prepared for what?" Baden-Powell, founder of the Scout movement, replied, "For any old thing." Wise fellow, BP. In my book "any old thing" definitely includes bones and treats.

People respond well to rewards. Everyone needs to be rewarded—sometimes with a big fat bone. (Or, in the case of humans, a nice check. Checks don't taste good though. I know. I've tried eating them.). Even Dr. Evil implored his son, Scott, to "throw me a frickin' bone here" when asking for recognition of evil deeds accomplished in the past. See what I mean? Even bad boys need to be rewarded—with bones no less!

THOUGHT TWELVE

To Sniff, or Not to Sniff: That is the Question
~ *Instinct*

Animals rely on instinct to survive and evolve—but I think *your* fine natural instincts have been destroyed by the preponderance of ill-conceived management commands, meetings, and reviews.

For example, in many companies, too often mistakes are punished quickly and decisively. This strong-willed, top-down management style is often interpreted as decisive leadership—but we dogs know better. Fear of reprisals engendered by leadership moves down the line—and unhealthy fear then becomes part of a company's culture. I believe that use of fear to subjugate members of a professional team is foolish in today's business environment. If you corner an animal, and they fear you, the animal will attack—sometimes viscously and often unexpectedly. Be warned if you run your company through iron-fisted fear.

Leadership comes from the top and derives from example. In some companies the fear of making a mistake or looking foolish is so overwhelming that it creates paralysis. I overheard someone telling Pam and Barry: "Nobody has ever been fired for saying or doing nothing in our company. Most of us don't do anything—and so we keep our jobs." This sounds like the movie *Office Space*! (I like to watch movies with Barry.) What a sad reflection on employee-management relations!

There are several potential outcomes at a company where such poor communications exists. First, supervisors are likely to search for scapegoats when things go wrong—particularly if the supervisor fears for *his* job. Second, employees will try to cover up mistakes rather than reveal them straight away—but no one likes surprises and misdeeds are almost always detected eventually. The consequences for individuals and companies are always worse when mistakes are not dealt with immediately. Third, trust will cease to exist among employees at all levels—and, without trust, leadership cannot survive for long. Fourth, and perhaps most devastating, no one in the company will be encouraged to take risks: Professional instinct flies out the window.

I've barked many times about how some of the greatest leaders in the world made mistakes—but then used those mistakes as examples to improve and succeed. Those who have never made a mistake—or, really, never *admitted* to making mistakes—may survive but will never thrive as leaders. Life itself is a risk and a risk-free existence isn't possible. One can take every precaution—and yet gremlins are everywhere. (Sometimes, when Katie or Reign bark at something unseen, I worry they see the gremlins!) Advances are made only by those willing to take risks. Great leaders follow their instincts. Great leaders do not always trust everyone or everything—but they trust themselves.

Barry often talks about the stories of extraordinary advances made during the world wars. The risks were often enormous and many mistakes were made—but the potential rewards for all of mankind were incalculable. Barry postulates that perhaps the biggest risks during those stressful times were not taking risks.

Barry was always impressed with his friend, Juergen. As the saying goes, Juergen was always "comfortable in his own skin." Juergen never hesitated to make decisions by following his personal instincts. Juergen's success rate was very high—even though, sometimes, those decisions, at first blush, appeared to fly in the face of logic, common sense, and management trend reports. Juergen's decisions were based on *calculated* risk; in other words, he was thoughtful and never reckless. Juergen also had a backup plan or a stepped approach (he called them "baby steps") that would provide flexibility for change as strategies and plans were implemented. I suspect the philosophy of calculated risk (with backup plans) has been employed by many great leaders.

How often have we read about successful entrepreneurs who made a decision about a product or service that appeared, at first glance, to have little chance of success? A decision based only on logic assumes all the facts are available, but my experience has taught me that one rarely knows every fact needed to make a cast-iron conclusion. There is an element of chance in life! To use one of my favorite aphorisms: If the bone smells and tastes bad, then don't eat the bone!

I could go on and on about when I've ignored my instincts and took action based solely on logic—but, in retrospect, I know now I lacked critical information. For example, there is the story about a piece of meat, a dog whom I suspected was no longer nearby, and a door that I knew nothing about … but I will go no further here as the memories are too painful.

Barry said he made some poor choices when he first became a unit manager. On several occasions, well-meaning staff presented factual information that made the decision appear obvious—but, in his heart, Barry knew something wasn't right. He should have trusted his instincts! He later discovered a key piece of information was missing from the initial report; his instincts would have been confirmed had that missing information been available. Should the staff have been more diligent in their research? Sometimes life does not allow the luxury of time to check every line of investigation; indeed, sometimes a delayed decision is as bad, or worse, than no decision.

We must trust ourselves—and this can be a difficult lesson to learn. Many people are afflicted by low self-esteem or a lack of self-confidence—but belief in yourself is critical in the business world. Believe or not, even dogs and horses can suffer from a lack of self-trust—but a good companion, trainer, or coach can help develop self-confidence. Pam is regularly called to help creatures who have lost trust in themselves or others, have low self-esteem, and lack confidence to face the world. Often these are rescue animals where human abuse is the root cause of the problem. Sometimes the problems manifest in aggression and fear of humans or other animals. Time, persistence, and patience are critical therapies when resolving these issues.

Be aware, however, that an over-reliance on instinct and self-belief can lead to an arrogance that can also result in problems. Your decision-making will suffer if you stop listening to others or ignore advice simply because you think you know better. Moreover, your colleagues will start to lose respect for you. In the animal kingdom, overconfidence and arrogance can lead to serious injury—or even death..

"A dog can't think that much about what he's doing, he just does what feels right." Collecting facts is sensible—but don't let facts rule the day. Follow your heart. You may not always be right—but you must learn to take risks.

Try to work for companies or bosses that respect calculated, well-considered risks—and bosses who trust their instincts. View mistakes as learning opportunities. Learn about great leaders who believed in themselves and triumphed despite adversity.

Be open to advice and counsel—and encourage open dialogue among colleagues. Remember: People are led by leaders, not bullies. To quote a friend of mine, A. Nonny-Mouse: "I dream of a better tomorrow, where chickens can cross the road and not be questioned about their motives." Dogs never question the motives of a chicken. We know instinctively, as do most animals, never to count your chickens before they hatch. I must confess, though, that I do love a nice piece of chicken with my meal—and that's why I never question them about what makes them tick. If I did that, then I would have to think about what life means to them—and I would not be able to enjoy my meal!

THOUGHT THIRTEEN

I'm Stuck on You
~ *Loyalty*

I was reading a quote from Tigress Luv (a relationship expert who is sometimes known as the "Breakup Guru"): "He then created the dog and with this new life He gave the dog His most treasured traits. ... unending loyalty, trust, faith, and unconditional love. This He did for man." I love this sentiment—although we canines know that, in fact, *The Great Dane* created dog in *Her* own image. Man was simply lucky enough to be on the receiving end of the Great Dane's conception.

What makes us so special to mankind? Our unbreakable and unquenchable loyalty to our human companions. Dogs remain ever-faithful and supportive—often in the face of man's cruelty and selfishness. A dog does not judge. He has no care about how a person might look or how intelligent (or otherwise) he or she may be. When all else fails in your life, your dog will be by your side. You might say we are loyal to a fault.

Humans can learn lessons from their canine friends—particularly as these lessons apply to a business environment. I do not mean to advise, however, that you should exhibit blind loyalty to your company. If, for example, you know of immoral or illegal acts, do not stay through "thick and thin" (a 10th-century saying, by the way, that derives from when England was a heavily forested land and finding your way through the woods was an art. The original saying was "through thicket and thin wood," meaning that you will find your way through the dense forests no matter what. Should the modern equivalent be "though traffic jam and leafy lane?" I like trees, however, and assist them to grow by watering them whenever I can).

Employee "loyalty" is becoming rarer. I suppose this is not surprising since so many companies nowadays display little loyalty to their employees. We have seen many companies fail to demonstrate any care about those who work for them. As we have noted, leadership starts at the top, so when companies act in the best interests of the business with little regard for those that serve them, they should hardly be surprised when loyalty is low. Still, shockingly, many companies expect unfettered loyalty from their employees. You humans have so many double standards!

Loyalty comes naturally to dogs—so I can't understand why people often view loyalty as a weakness rather than a strength. Loyalty, in my wonderfully non-human opinion, should be regarded with respect and cherished as a gift rather than as part of an employment contract. Loyalty is an act of the heart and mind. In the human world, as with respect, loyalty is earned—and is not an expectation. Dan Gemeinhart, author of *The Honest Truth*, wrote: "Dogs die. But dogs live, too. Right up until they die, they live. They live brave, beautiful lives. They protect their families. And love us. And make our lives a little brighter. And they don't waste time being afraid of tomorrow." This is true—and brings quite a tear to this emotional canine's eye.

Companies should realize that customer and employee loyalty is worth its weight in gold (literally), so treating this gift with respect and love is a sensible thing to do. So many businesses today act as though their customers should be grateful for whatever they get—but the best marketing advice suggests that customer retention is a key factor to success. One recent survey I pawed through pointed out that 96 percent of unhappy customers do not complain; they simply tell between 9 to

20 other people about their bad experience! Eighty-seven percent of those who hear about another consumer's bad experience never make a purchase from that company. Additionally, the original customer, having spread the bad word, is 91 percent certain never to buy from the company again. The same survey estimates that it costs five times more to attract new customers than to keep existing ones—and that 82 percent to 95 percent of customers will buy again from a company that resolves any issues to the customer's satisfaction.

I believe that it's not always what you do, or don't do, that affects the outcome with a customer, but rather the way you react when you are made aware of a problem. We know that mistakes happen—and customers forgive if a mistake is recognized, responsibility accepted, and the error rectified in an appropriate and timely fashion. Pam told me she sticks with companies that support her concerns—safe in the knowledge that mistakes will be corrected should anything go wrong. She is a loyal customer to companies who return that loyalty—and she tells others about her experiences, too.

Customer loyalty is worth a lot of money. One estimate I saw calculated that it costs a company $17,000 to replace a lost customer who spent $1,000 per year with that company. I'm never quite sure who calculates these numbers or how they are determined—but the message is clear: Customer retention, satisfaction, and loyalty are critical to the success of any business. Doesn't that just make business cents (for a dog that probably should be scents)? My advice is to ensure the penny drops (an English saying that derived from the sound made by the mechanism of a penny in a slot machines; perhaps the closest phrase in the United States is "the light bulb turns on") for everyone in the company.

I've talked about how everyone matters in a company—from the CEO down. Loyalty matters, too. Imagine how much more enjoyable the workplace can be if everyone in the company understands the impact they can have on themselves, their fellow employees, their company results, and their customers. Loyal employees, loyal to serving the customer to the best of their abilities, attract and retain loyal customers.

The D.E.V. is obvious: Dogs are naturally loyal companions. We know that loyalty is a strength and not a weakness. Even those business skeptics who are interested only in their personal well-being should understand that loyalty contributes to their best self-interests. I have always placed a very high value on loyalty and have found my loyalty to others is rewarded by their loyalty to me. When times are difficult, or situations to be faced are tough, the loyalty of my friends and family have invariably seen me through adversity. Those who are disloyal to others will be shunned, feared, or mistrusted. I know that displaying loyalty can sometimes be difficult—loyalty can sometimes require great courage and effort—but the benefits speak for themselves.

And you are a loyal reader if you have made it thus far: Thank you! I appreciate your loyalty and I offer you a long-distance pat on the head, a scratch behind the ears, a rub on your tummy, and some petting on your bottom. Feels good, doesn't it? If you continue to the end, perhaps we could play some catch? You know one of my favorite people is Doris Day. I loved her even more when she said: "I have found that when you are deeply troubled, there are things you get from the silent devoted companionship of a dog that you can get from no other source." That's how dogs often show their loyalty: quietly.

THOUGHT FOURTEEN

My Nose Is Twitching
~ *Sensitivity*

Animals are so much more sensitive than humans on a physical plane but we are less complex emotionally. In this dog's modest—but acutely intelligent and perceptive—opinion, animals are more balanced than humans. On the physical side, for example, dogs and horses are much more sensitive than humans to touch, and some dogs are ten thousand times more sensitive to smell.

Merlin told me he can hear low-frequency sounds much better than humans, he can turn his ears 180 degrees by using 10 different muscles, he can taste things more acutely, his sense of smell is way better, and he can feel a fly on a single hair. Humans, on the other hand, leap about like a rabid goat only after they've been bitten by some bug like a mosquito—slapping themselves in the vain hope of hitting the biter who long ago moved on to a new human victim.

In addition, animals normally don't harbor grudges. We forgive easily (except in the case of cats, who do harbor grudges and never forgive!)—and we don't lie, hate, cheat, or gossip.

Our superior sense of touch can be used to help us, too! As part of her initial training into the world of animal massage, energy work, healing, and therapy, Pam, with Barry in attendance for support, attended a couple of clinics concerning a particular method relating to horse wellness and comfort. Jim, the gentleman running this school, had developed a hands-on method over many years that involved finding tight or restricted areas on a horse and then releasing them. For example, he would run his hands lightly on either side of the horse's spine and other parts of the body. Jim would stop if the horse blinked several times—as blinking signified an issue. He would hold in this area until the horse started to yawn, fidget, lick, or chew—as these were signs that the horse was releasing tension.

Pam and Barry also traveled to Hawaii to attend a training course on caring for animals through touch and love. (Barry said someone had to assist Pam and, to my complete disgust, they left me behind.) Linda, the lady running these courses, holds separate sessions for horses, dogs, and humans. (I would think that the course for humans is very difficult for Linda to teach considering their lack of sensitivity!) Upon their return, Barry told me they had witnessed some remarkable results from using Linda's teaching.

For example, Barry said that Linda was introduced to a horse who had recently arrived at the barn. The mare was very unsettled and fiery—she would rear into the air with front forelegs flailing when someone approached—and the owners thought they might have to let her go. Linda slowly and quietly moved toward the horse, all the while talking gently. She was soon using her TTouch® method to soothe and calm the horse. Incredibly, a short while later, Linda led the horse into the arena, mounted, and rode the animal around the track. Linda then continued teaching the course with the horse standing calmly by her side. When the horse returned to the stable, instead of trying to nip and bite other horses around her, the mare simply looked around before contentedly munching on her hay. Barry was stunned (and it takes a lot to stun Barry!).

Linda believes that students who take her course will be able to "… understand and influence your animal with your heart and hands in a way that develops trust, creates a harmonious relationship, and changes unwanted behavior." Linda described the science behind her methods during her lessons. She talked about the number of highly respected academic institutions she had worked with over the years that had conducted studies and research into why her methods worked. Linda's work has been endorsed by some of the top scientists in their profession.

Pam is also an extraordinary animal healer. She has many modalities in her tool box to serve and heal four-legged critters. Pam is also a certified Healing Touch for Animals® (HTA) practitioner, and she uses HTA at the core of her practice to improve an animal's health, comfort, quality of life, mental and emotional state, and to increase and enhance the animal/human bond. HTA is a series of techniques developed by our friend, Carol, to assist animals to restore natural self-healing and provide a state of balance through energetic connections and the application of energy medicine. Carol always begins by explaining to her students that an animal has a sensitive energy field many times greater than humans. For example, Carol advises that horses have an energy field ten times greater than homo sapiens. This probably explains why I can never get near enough to a cat or a mouse without them being aware of my intentions.

Barry says he can only stand and marvel at the many wonders he has been privileged to witness Pam perform during the course of her ministrations. Pam has an amazing ability to understand both the physical and emotional needs of animals. He says it's rather like watching the 1964 Walt Disney film, *Mary Poppins*, starring Julie Andrews, where she digs into her never-ending bag and digs out just the right remedy for any problem.

Thinking about Jim, Linda, Carol, Pam, and others set me to ponder whether these same sorts of treatments could be employed to work on human emotional sensitivity—particularly as this relates to the emotional pains and agonies you all appear to suffer at work.

How do these animal folks achieve such profound results?

1. They establish bonds of trust.
The practitioners all use doses of gentleness and understanding—not anger and a whip. This is not to say the teachers were slow to admonish misbehavior—but firm leadership was never established through hitting and shouting. To quote the philosopher Dagobert D. Runes: "You cannot train a horse with shouts and expect it to obey a whisper."

2. They identify the root of any problem.
Linda, for example, quickly established that the behavior of the

"dangerous" horse was driven by the uncertainty and fear of new surroundings, people, and other horses. The horse exhibited aggression and unruly behavior, but Linda recognized this behavior was a symptom, not the cause of why the horse was misbehaving.

3. They develop smart strategies to heal or change behaviors.
Through observation, experience, and understanding the practitioners will determine what they want to achieve when working with an animal. For example, Linda wanted to establish the troubling horse as a dependable member of the barn by removing its fear and uncertainty though reassurance and trust.

4. They develop and implement precise tactics.
The best tactics require constant review. All of the practitioners discussed above consistently modify their plans in recognition of the animals' strengths, weaknesses, environment, health, issues, and concerns.

5. They create unwavering and confident leadership.
A hesitant leader cannot work with fearful and uncertain animals. Rewards are quickly established for good animal behavior. At every training event that I've attended, instructors always encourage students to reward their animals with either praise or food for jobs well done. Believe me—that works for me!

6. They are prepared to patiently await the result.
Leaders instinctively know it takes time, patience, and persistence to ensure the best results. As John Heywood, the English playwright, once wrote: "Rome wasn't built in a day, but they were laying bricks every hour." When training my humans, I find that I need to patiently repeat actions many times for them to finally understand what I need them to do. Humans can be very dense at times, so I try not to lose my temper with them. That said, these animal leaders instinctively understand when an animal has had enough for the day. Pushing an animal past it's limits only negates positive results achieved.

If business managers would implement some of these lessons, they would be more respected by subordinates, peers, and superiors—

and feel better about themselves, too! We must encourage these management tips! Let us howl together by yowling the famous Peter, Paul and Mary song: "Go *tell* it on the mountain, over the hills and everywhere."

The D.E.V.: The best results are achieved through strong leadership, where a leader identifies strengths and weaknesses in an individual, and is prepared to be flexible in approach. Remember: Encouragement and rewards (treats!) work better than punishment.

THOUGHT FIFTEEN

The Last Lick

We have reached the end of this short journey. I hope that I have convinced you that animals have so much more to offer than mankind! We are generous of spirit, kind in nature, warm of heart, loyal to a fault, and smart as a whip (which alludes to the sharpness of the sound a whip when cracked—often above a horse [which is why Merlin hates this saying!]).

I like to tell this little story, by the renowned novelist and historian Edmund Fuller, to better illustrate how highly we dogs are thought of by some innovative and intelligent people:

> "Thomas A. Edison was once reluctantly persuaded by his wife to attend one of the big social functions of the season in New York. At last the inventor managed to escape the crowd of people vying for his attention, and sat alone unnoticed in a corner. Edison kept looking at his watch with a resigned expression on his face. A friend edged near to him unnoticed and heard the inventor mutter to himself with a sigh, 'If there were only a dog here!' "

Of course, Merlin would not let me get away with simply relating this one valuable tale. He had to go one better and insisted I add a quote from William Shakespeare's *Henry V* describing thoughts about a horse. William Shakespeare no less! Merlin is such a literary snob! I relate the quote here since Merlin is bigger than me:

> *"He's of the colour of the nutmeg. And of the heat of the ginger…he is pure air and fire; and the dull elements of earth and water never appear in him, but only in patient stillness while his rider mounts him; he is indeed a horse, and all other jades you may call beasts."*

I know that "jades" refers to broken-down, vicious, or worthless horses, but Merlin made it clear he translates this to mean that it refers to any other creature than a horse. He wants to call all other creatures "beasts"? Merlin may find that, as stated in Proverbs 16:18: "Pride goeth before destruction, and a haughty spirit before a fall." When the backlash comes, size is not everything.

The good news? There is hope for mankind—if you are all willing to listen and learn from your animal companions. As the humorist, author, and screenwriter Corey Ford wrote: "Properly trained, a man can be dog's best friend." I agree! I have faith that my human friends can and will do better—despite all their faults!

Through the wonders of modern media, we see and hear every day about many bad things happening in the world. We cannot, and should not, ignore or downplay these events—but, even from my lowly position, I also see so many good things happening! For example, I know that many humans are turning to more natural foods and are beginning to care more for their environment. Humans are also beginning to accept non-traditional paths to heal themselves.

Since I love horses (and I know that Pam and Barry love horses), I am aware that there are a number of well-respected horse trainers, such as Pam's riding instructor, Jennifer Bauer, who, along with her mentor Larry Whitesell, have been perfecting natural horsemanship techniques for many years. These amazing trainers share their knowledge to the benefit of both riders and horses. Jennifer used to give lessons to Barry, too, when Ramo was alive. I am surprised Barry managed to stay in the saddle, but Jennifer demonstrated the patience of a saint and never shouted at him or gave up trying. Ramo attempted to follow Barry's confusing requests as best he could, but you could tell from Ramo's frequent, longing glances toward the barn how he felt about the whole endeavor.

A good friend of ours, Buddy Brewer, provides fascinating insights as to how to effectively communicate with horses by using the language of the horse. Buddy uses techniques developed by Chris Irwin to "sensitize people" to connect with the many counter-intuitive nuances of the mind of the horse so the horse can truly understand, appreciate, and willingly cooperate with humans.

The methods developed by such trainers prove that wonderful and rewarding results for both humans and horses can be achieved with patience, belief, and hard work. Think about what these trainers bring to the party: Both the riders and the horses enjoy their experiences—because they are all having fun!

If there is horsemanship, then there must be "dogmanship"—and, today, there are thousands of books on the subject. I always love this comment from world-famous dog behaviorist Cesar Millan: "I have never met a dog I couldn't help; however, I have met humans who weren't willing to change."

I am also pleased that we smaller creatures have not been neglected in the area of natural health. Some years ago, the University of Tennessee started an Integrative Medicine Department (IMD) for small animals. At the time, I was in real trouble with my ears and feet because of some pretty serious issues with allergies—spring, summer, and fall. Then Pam heard about a vet at the UT IMD—and I met an angel named Dr. Donna Raditic. Dr. Donna, as her human clients affectionately call her, soon helped me with a special diet and a host of natural recommendations that Pam and Barry could implement to help me. Katie and Reign became patients, too! Dr. Donna has a devoted following through her use of natural solutions, combining both Eastern and Western methods with amazing results.

The Integrative Medicine Department at UT was shut down,

ostensibly due to lack of funds—but, before she left, clients held a going-away party in honor of Dr. Donna. There were many gifts, but I was most touched by the many clients who talked about how Dr, Donna and her staff had saved their dog's lives. These were people who loved their pets and were unwilling to give up on them when other traditional treatments had failed. Dr. Donna was often the last port of call for these animals. Dr. Donna did not seem to mind in the least and would always joke that the dogs would raise a paw and say "Not dead yet!" Each poignant story brought a new flood of tears—and joy and laughter, too! Time and again, people expressed their thanks, not just for the treatment of their friends, but for the loving and gentle care provided by Dr. Donna. Now, through her animal therapy work, Pam has been privileged to be able to work on some of Dr. Donna's patients in support of Dr. Donna's methods and treatments. Pam still visits several of these pets, years after Dr. Donna had initially treated the animals.

I've written about people such as Linda Tellington-Jones, and her TTouch® method; Jim Masterson, who developed The Masterson Method®; and Carol Komitor and her Healing Touch for Animals®. All of these remarkable healers bring love and comfort to people and their animals. Linda's work has at its roots "… a philosophy that sees all beings—humans and animals alike—as reflections of a Divine Whole." Jim's philosophy is best summed up here: "It is something you do with the horse, rather than to the horse." And Carol writes: "Are you ready to make a difference? Well, are you? I so hope so."

Such insightfulness fills me with hope. My companion and friend, Pam, has used her natural methods and techniques countless times to rejuvenate and improve the health and well-being of so many animals (including birds and goats!). I know mankind can succeed! Follow these fearless leaders! Their journey has not always been easy. They have faced many trials and tribulations, many doubters, and many people who have criticized their efforts—yet they have risen above all and triumphed. Try to apply "natural workmanship" techniques at your workplace so you, too, can have fun every day. At least one-third of your time will improve beyond measure.

You must believe in yourself and others. All too often natural talents such as kindness, respect, generosity, patience, sensitivity, instinct, empathy, compassion, optimism, trust, playfulness, enthusiasm, and humor are viewed in the business world as weaknesses. Trust this canine: They are strengths! Remember, too, that, as someone once said, the reason dogs have so many friends is because they wag their tails instead of their tongues.

Be and feel passionate about your work. Communicate your passion to the world—and don't be ashamed to sing from the rooftops! Take pride in who you are and what you do. Be guided by your instincts. Above all: Enjoy what you do and don't be afraid to have fun doing it.

A Final Note: Let me know how you get on and whether these thoughts have helped. Remember: We must communicate in order to succeed both individually and collectively. I'm only a bark, growl, whine, or howl away. And feel free to send me spare bones or treats; I am happy to dispose of them in a natural way on your behalf.

May your nose remain wet, may you shed hair without mess, may your tail keep wagging, and may your Great Dane (or whatever breed to which you are devoted) be with you.

Dog bless,
Parker Stanner the Third.

Acknowledgements

I used to enjoy writing some odd stories for friends, family, and myself—just short stories about some of my experiences. My wife, Pam, was the first to suggest I write a book. I was flattered—but I did not immediately put pen to paper. Then, one day, we went to a book signing in Knoxville. At the end of his session, the author brought his coffee over to where Pam and I were enjoying a small repast. He asked if we had ever thought about writing a book. I laughed, but Pam told the author she wanted me to write a book and that I would not take her seriously. The author leaned toward me, grabbed my wrist, looked me straight in the eyes, and uttered these fateful words "Everyone has at least one good book in them."

I told him I had no talent for writing, and he responded that by "good book" he meant one that was satisfying for the author to read—it didn't matter if anybody else liked it. Well, most appropriately for these ramblings, that was like throwing a dog a bone as far as Pam was concerned. She glowed triumphantly, and I knew I was in trouble.

We later went to visit with our dear friend and mentor, Bobby Drinnon. Bobby was often labeled by those who did not understand him as a clairvoyant, psychic, prophet, seer, or mystic. Bobby never claimed any of these titles; instead he chose "intuitive counselor." He did, in truth, provide uncannily accurate counsel—but Pam and I have always believed that Bobby's mission was to help people better understand themselves, to teach them ways to improve, and to find paths that would allow them and others to lead a better and happier existence.

On one particular visit, Bobby told me that I needed to start writing a book. The suggestion had Pam bouncing in her chair. Bobby made me promise I would one day settle down to at least write something. I was then in full-time employment, did not think I had any talent for writing, and somehow time slipped away. Every time Pam and I saw Bobby, he would remind me of my promise. In the back of my mind I did keep thinking about it. I mentioned to Bobby that I had an idea that I would pen a book that would be written by our Vizsla dog, Parker. Bobby stared into space for a short while, gave one of his radiant smiles, and said, "Yes, you will." Pam (pun intended) hounded me over the years to keep my promise to Bobby.

When I retired mid-way through 2013, Pam insisted that I no longer had any excuses. I was still uncertain about my writing ability and had a host of projects to complete that had been put off over the years. Then, about seven months into my retirement, I felt I should at last make a start on the book.

We knew that Bobby had been ill with cancer for some time, but had seen him in the late fall of the previous year when he seemed to be responding well to some experimental treatment. Early in 2014, both Pam and I started to get an uneasy feeling that all was not well with Bobby. We tried calling but could never reach him. As spring drew near the intensity to write a book grew, to the point where it was starting to become an obsession. For reasons I could not explain, I felt an overwhelming urgency to get it done. I was about two-thirds of the way through the first draft when we received a call to let us know that Bobby had only a short time to live. We were devastated. A short while later, on March 3, 2014, Bobby crossed his rainbow bridge to the place where he is meant to be.

I am neither cynical nor given to flights of fancy. Pam has extraordinary healing abilities and insights about life; despite Pam's protestations to the contrary, I liken myself to a dead piece of wood. I am convinced, however, that Bobby had decided I would write my book, and we were going to get it done one way or the other. I believe, along with Pam, he was both the inspiration and the driving force behind the completion of this project. With those two together, what chance did I stand? Pam and I still feel Bobby's presence around us.

~ Bobby Drinnon was a man of light—and with his passing the world became a darker place. During his lifetime, Bobby helped many people, including Pam and me. He saved lives, guided souls lost in the black depths of despair to return to the sunshine, and provided inspiration, strength, and courage to so many of those he touched. Bobby's faith in God and in people never wavered. To Bobby: Thank you.

~ My wife, friend, and soul mate, Pam, has been both a major influence in my life and the reason for my existence. We met later in life, but when both of us look back we believe there was a reason for this. When you are younger, you do not always appreciate all the things around you. Pam and I fell in love the moment we met, and so it has remained. We live our lives as one, a concept not always readily understood by many. She provided the courage for me to write. Her patience and support during the writing of this book and other scribblings that will follow has been incredible. When I doubted myself, Pam did not. I shall be eternally grateful to her for this, and so many other things, too.

~ Thank you to all my friends and family for their wonderful support, for making suggestions for changes, and, most of all, for not laughing at me. A special thanks to my brother. Throughout my life he has been my brother, friend, mentor, supporter, and tennis coach. I once beat him at tennis after many hundreds of attempts. I had to be patient until he was seriously injured and over 70, but it was worth the wait.

~ Thank you to my friend, Juergen Stein, who gave me so much insight about how work can really be a joy rather than a drudge, and that happiness in life really can be up to you. Juergen is a true leader. Although technically brilliant, with a sharp and insightful mind, Juergen has a wonderful sense of humor, loves doing fun things, and is definitely a people person. He values trust, loyalty, honesty, and the opinions of others. He is a rare breed. Where others have processes, Juergen has vision and instinct.

~ Thank you to Ann Walden. I think Ann knows everyone on the planet, and has been a friend to Pam for more years than either probably want to remember. Ann introduced me to Larry Perry and then Martha Woodward. Apart from being a very interesting person to meet, Larry's advice as an author himself helped me to understand what I was letting myself in for. Martha took my ramblings and helped me begin to cast them into a format that other human beings had a chance of understanding. She also taught me few lessons about how to shorten sentences and coached me in the use of antecedents.

~ Thank you to Steven Friedlander, my editor, who has become a firm friend and guide. Without his ability to steer me through the complexities of publishing, his consistent correction of my grammar and formatting, and his knowledge of the industry, I doubt this book would ever have been completed. Steven brought professionalism and a healthy dose of realism to my writings. He injected some common sense into the prose and tried to teach me about the process of publishing a book. I'm not sure that last gift stuck too well—but he has been very patient. Steven's guidance and honesty are very much appreciated.

This book was inspired by, to some degree, *The Hitchhikers Guide to the Galaxy*. I heartily recommend reading the series, and I suggest you have some fun by viewing the film. I can still remember waiting avidly for the BBC television series of *HHGTTG* to be screened each week. When Douglas Adams wrote the scripts for the BBC series back in the 1970s, it always seemed to me he was writing about the nonsense of life and how we take ourselves far too seriously. Look at things a different way and you change the outcome. I hope this philosophy shines through in Parker's writings.

Roy Spence's book, *It's Not What You Sell, It's What You Stand For*, helped clarify and put sense to many of the business values I have held for most of my life.

I would be remiss not to recognize the considerable contribution to making the world a happier place for both horses and horse lovers provided by Jim Masterson, Jennifer Bauer, Larry Whitesell, and, more lately, Buddy Brewer. These folks are helping humans to understand more about how to care for, work with, and communicate to their equine friends. To put it simply, this is an amazing group of people with outstanding gifts.

Dr. Donna Raditic and her partner, Dr. Joe Bartges, have helped many animals, as well as many dog and cat owners, to rise above horrible circumstances and triumphantly lead a better quality of life and happiness. Dr. D's patience and love for both animals and people is a shining example of what can be achieved through science, patience, kindness, an open heart, and, above all, respect for all creatures.

Linda Tellington-Jones is an extraordinary woman. She and her husband, Roland, travel the world so that Linda can impart her wonderful gift of touch and compassion to animals and humans alike. Apart from her outstanding books, videos, and teachings, Linda's very presence and enthusiasm lift and invigorate a person's joy of life and determination to do better. She truly is inspirational.

Carol Komitor is responsible for bringing the amazing methods of healing, developed for people by Janet Mentgen, to the world of animals. Carol founded Healing Touch for Animals® in 1996 and her dedication to the processes she has developed over time is extraordinary. Carol has repeatedly shown how energy work and essential oils can bring healing, great comfort, and wellness to animals (and their human companions). Unlike humans, animals have no agenda, and are happy to soak up the benefits this work provides. Carol is an extraordinary person in so many different ways. She runs her own animal healing practice, teaches students around the world how to develop and use skills for energy work most of us fail to recognize we possess, and mentors those around her to pass on the knowledge she has developed. She also provides comfort and understanding to pet lovers in a way that empowers them to bring the care of animals to a new level, and, above all, has provided a new quality of life to countless animals.

Carol and Walter Sommerfelt, Vizsla breeders, dog show organizers, handlers, and judges extraordinaire, breed their dogs not just for their beautiful looks but also for their amazing temperament. It is no accident that their dogs are the most loving, best-tempered Vizslas around. The Sommerfelt family spend many hours socializing and looking after the puppies long before they are passed on to their final homes. Puppies are very carefully selected to suit the people and their reasons for wanting one of the Sommerfelt dogs. Anyone who just wants to buy a "cute dog" will be out of luck. Parker was our first dog to come from Carol and Wally. We were lucky to have found them (well, Pam found them actually) and for the Sommerfelts to agree we could own one of their dogs.

I urge you to learn more about these fine people and their methods.

Meeting and working with these folks has been a true privilege for Pam and me. They have been the inspiration behind some of the stories and ideas in this and future books on ways to lead a more fulfilling, happier life. Thank goodness people like this exist in our world; they lead the way to understanding and enlightenment for all of us.

My final acknowledgement: To the "author" of this book. Parker was our first Vizsla. He is a very special boy. He seems to have an amazing effect on all who meet him, and his genuine joy when greeting people is infectious. Pam searched for a long time to find a dog breed she thought would fit into our household. One day, after many intense hours of research, Pam simply announced she felt in her heart that we needed a Vizsla. "A whatta?" I responded intelligently. Pam then started to research breeders, a task more daunting than she had expected. Finally, to our amazement, she was told of a highly respected breeder of Vizslas not far from where were living.

The rest is history. I was somewhat skeptical about getting another dog so soon after we had lost one of our beloved rescue dogs to cancer. Then I met Rudy, Parker's dad, and that was the end of that! We now share two other Vizslas with Carol and Wally. Reign, our second Vizsla, became a Grand Champion thanks to Carol and Wally's handling expertise—and she has since given birth to several litters of wonderful puppies, many of them champions in their own right.

A puppy from one of Reign's litters, Katie, joined the Stanner family a few years ago—and she is a delightful addition to the household. We call them the Vizslateers" since they really do follow Alexandre Dumas's *Three Musketeers* motto of "One for all, and all for one." Be warned, though: These dogs carry a health warning about addiction if you like loving, beautiful, intelligent, cuddly dogs. Once you have owned a Vizsla you are highly likely to become a Vizsla junkie. Don't take my word for it: Ask any Vizsla owner—but be sure you have a cup of coffee and are sitting in a comfortable chair before you do so. There are so many stories to tell!

About The Author

Barry Stanner is a retired business manager. He was born in North London, where he spent his formative years. Barry's first job in 1963 was as an indentured apprentice instrument maker with the Cambridge Instrument Company. During his five-year apprenticeship he attended the University of Enfield, where he received his engineering certification. He spent six- to eight-month rotations in each department of the company. Barry gained a great deal of experience in how each department operated and functioned. He also acquired an understanding of the different resources, types of people, and skills required for each department to be successful.

Barry joined the American based company, EG&G, in 1976. The company provided advanced scientific instrumentation to the nuclear research industry. He held a variety of management positions during his 28 years with EG&G, including Managing Director of the UK operations, a position he held for over 10 years. In 1997, he relocated to the divisional headquarters in Oak Ridge, Tennessee, as Vice President of Sales and Marketing.

In January of 2003, Barry formed a subsidiary company in the United States on behalf of his friend and company owner, Juergen Stein. The new company, Target Instruments, designed, manufactured, and distributed hand-held nuclear radiation devices for the homeland security market. Based in Oak Ridge, the company grew quickly and was soon the market leader in the United States. The company was later sold to a larger corporate organization.

Barry became a citizen of the United States in 2011—some years after meeting and marrying his best friend, love of his life, and soul mate, Pamela. They live with their three Vizsla dogs, Parker, Reign, and Katie, alongside Merlin, Pam's Paso Fino horse, in beautiful East Tennessee. Barry still likes to travel to the United Kingdom to visit his son Michael and husband Andrew; daughter Joanne and husband Matt; their wonderful grandchildren, Ethan and Henry; and Barry's greatest life buddy, his brother John, and his wife, Pauline.

Barry and his family (including Parker, of course) can be reached at: *barrystanner@gmail.com.*